entertaining
at home

entertaining at home

over 65 sensational sure-fire recipes
for successful dinner parties, lunches,
celebrations and buffets

contributing editor
bridget **jones**

southwater

This edition is published by Southwater,
an imprint of Anness Publishing Ltd,
Hermes House, 88–89 Blackfriars Road, London SE1 8HA;
tel. 020 7401 2077; fax 020 7633 9499

www.southwaterbooks.com; www.annesspublishing.com

If you like the images in this book and would like to investigate using
them for publishing, promotions or advertising, please visit
our website www.practicalpictures.com for more information.

Publisher: Joanna Lorenz
Editorial Director: Helen Sudell
Senior Editors: Doreen Palamartschuk and Sarah Uttridge
Copy Editors: Jan Cutler and Jane Bamforth
Project Editor: Elizabeth Woodland
Production Controller: Claire Rae
Designer: Nigel Partridge
Jacket Design: Balley Design Associates
Photographers: Karl Adamson, Caroline Arber, Steve Baxter,
Martin Brigdale, Nicki Dowey, Gus Filgate, Michelle Garrett,
Amanda Heywood, Janine Hosegood, William Lingwood,
Roisin Neild, Thomas Odulate, Spike Powell, Craig Robertson,
Simon Smith, Sam Stowell and Polly Wreford

© Anness Publishing Ltd 2004, 2008

A CIP catalogue record for this book is available from the British Library.

UK agent: The Manning Partnership Ltd; tel. 01225 478444; fax 01225 478440; sales@manning-partnership.co.uk
UK distributor: Grantham Book Services Ltd; tel. 01476 541080; fax 01476 541061; orders@gbs.tbs-ltd.co.uk
North American agent/distributor: National Book Network; tel. 301 459 3366;
fax 301 429 5746; www.nbnbooks.com
Australian agent/distributor: Pan Macmillan Australia; tel. 1300 135 113;
fax 1300 135 103; customer.service@macmillan.com.au
New Zealand agent/distributor: David Bateman Ltd; tel. (09) 415 7664; fax (09) 415 8892

Previously published as part of a larger volume, *Party Food*

ETHICAL TRADING POLICY
Because of our ongoing ecological investment programme, you, as our customer, can have the pleasure and
reassurance of knowing that a tree is being cultivated on your behalf to naturally replace the materials used to
make the book you are holding. For further information about this scheme, go to www.annesspublishing.com/trees

Notes
Bracketed terms are intended for American readers.
For all recipes, quantities are given in both metric and imperial measures and,
where appropriate, measures are also given in standard cups and spoons.
Follow one set, but not a mixture, because they are not interchangeable.
Standard spoon and cup measures are level.
1 tsp = 5ml, 1 tbsp = 15ml, 1 cup = 250ml/8fl oz
Australian standard tablespoons are 20ml. Australian readers should
use 3 tsp in place of 1 tbsp for measuring small quantities of gelatine, flour, salt, etc.
Medium (US large) eggs are used unless otherwise stated.

contents

Introduction

Entertaining at home should be fun and there are many fantastic tips and recipes in this book to ensure success. All events and dinner parties are made easier with good forward planning, and the following advice will help make things run smoothly.

Record Keeping

Keeping records and notes makes social gatherings easier to plan. Take a sample planner from any personal organizer, or the computer equivalent, and adapt it to your needs.

Personal Party Organizer

Entertaining usually falls into two categories: professional and obligatory, or having fun with friends and family.

For most of us, occasions for seriously formal entertaining have greatly reduced. To be cost-effective, business entertaining and networking is generally planned by established principles – A, B and C list guests, dates and times, and style, are all decided according to known successes, and tweaking the system is all that's needed for variation.

More casual entertaining is easier and less formulaic; however, establishing a simple formula for sorting out essentials still saves time, gives confidence and allows everyone to enjoy themselves.

Files and Folders

Keep records on a computer or in a ring-binder or book. The advantage of computer files is that updating is easier. Start with three categories: planning, preparation and presentation. Sub-divide these to cater for all sorts of events and personal preferences.

Spreadsheet programs are ideal for recording most information, or you can draw tables. If sitting working at the computer is too tedious, print out blank charts or tables to fit your organizer. Alternatively, use an account book with columns, or draw tables by hand.

Right *Careful planning beforehand means that, on the day, you can relax and enjoy your party.*

Address Book

A well-organized address book is a social lifeline. It is the tool for making successful guest lists. Random jottings may be fun in a new book but the point of good records is that they are easy to access – ideally, use a spreadsheet program so that the contents can be organized by events or other columns as well as by name at the click of a mouse. Allow space for notes – people who get on brilliantly, vegetarian and special diets, food hates, and the names of friends' or neighbours' partners and children.

If you often have large get-togethers, keep a separate category of names and addresses of useful companies or suppliers. For example, specialist food and wine suppliers, caterers, catering companies, waiting staff, bar staff, washer-uppers, cleaning agencies for pre-party scrub-ups, gardeners who will come and tidy up outside, window cleaners, and local hotels or guest houses. Remember to include costs.

Above *A combination of good lighting and candles on the table will make for an elegant dinner party.*

Occasions

Keep a record of who came, when and for what: dates, times, number of guests and names, styles, themes, entertainment, type of food, drinks, decorations. Noting down details that are otherwise forgotten makes it easy to plan something similar again.

Food

The traditional formal menu book, with guest lists and descriptions of monumental dishes, served a practical purpose as a fast-track planning aid for future meals. In fact, menu records are even more useful today as there is so much choice. Courses do not have to be numerous or elaborate, but it's helpful to remind yourself of a brilliant combination of dips, dunks and goodies that made irresistible finger food, as well as any dishes that weren't such a big success. Useful categories to have could be snacks, finger food, buffets, dinner parties, quick suppers, barbecues and children's parties. Note down costs, preparation times, cook-ahead successes, fun foods to cook with friends, and so on.

Planning and Preparation

Successful entertaining involves some thought beforehand.

Impromptu Options

If ad-hoc invitations are your style, maintaining a constant stock of delicious things to eat is a good idea. Keep shopping lists and tick off items as they are used. Long-life items include ready-to-bake breads, jars or cans of olives, fish, marinated vegetables, bottled fruit, pasta, couscous, dried fruit and so on. Examples of foods that make it from frozen to table with minimum hassle include wraps, pancakes and unusual breads; thin or small pieces of fish, poultry or tender meat that cook quickly from frozen; easy vegetables for hot dishes or salads, such as baby broad beans; favourite ice creams or sorbets; and summer fruit.

Get-it-done Guide

Make a checklist of everything that needs doing:
• guest lists and invitations for larger or more formal occasions
• cleaning, tidying, clearing your refrigerator and freezer space
• shopping

• food preparation and cooking (ahead, on the day and last minute)
• special cooking arrangements – such as barbecues or coping with large amounts
• table setting and other presentation. Consider how long each task will take, ensure all is possible and have a realistic schedule for getting everything organized. Put deadlines against tasks that have to be completed well in advance. Enlist help and allocate jobs if necessary. Be slightly pessimistic rather than over-optimistic. Have a tick box for marking off completed items. Copies of successful schedules for big parties are invaluable for future reference even if the details are slightly modified for each event.

Shopping List

Start with the menu and numbers of guests, list the foods for each dish or course separately, then combine these into one list, for example, if eggs are used in three dishes. Make a note of the total cost – even if it is not exact, it allows for useful comparison between menus in future.

Above *Treat your party guests to a variety of freshly baked bread.*

Presentation

Think about the kind of ambience you want to create – especially for a special occasion or a themed party – when deciding on the following:
• invitations
• entertainment, from music (whether to get everyone dancing), to hiring professionals, such as magicians
• menu
• how to greet, introductions, and where to settle down, start and end the meal
• table settings and seating plans
• lighting, decor or decorations.

Above *Displaying menus at a dinner party is a great way of letting your guests know what they will be eating.*

Above *Create an exotic theme to a summer party with colourful and unusual drinks.*

brunches and lunches

Stylish dishes that are understated and easy to eat go down well for these light meal occasions, bringing a sophisticated touch to informal entertaining.

Scrambled Eggs with Smoked Salmon

For a luxury brunch, you cannot beat this special combination. Try it with a glass of champagne or sparkling wine mixed with freshly squeezed orange juice.

Serves 8

8 slices of pumpernickel or wholemeal (whole-wheat) bread, crusts trimmed
115g/4oz/½ cup butter
250g/9oz thinly sliced smoked salmon
12 eggs
90–120ml/6–8 tbsp double (heavy) cream
120ml/8 tbsp crème fraîche
salt and ground black pepper
generous 120ml/8 tbsp lumpfish roe or salmon caviar and sprigs of dill, to garnish

VARIATION
Another real treat is to grate a little fresh truffle into the scrambled eggs.

1 Spread the slices of bread with half of the butter and put on to eight individual plates. Arrange the smoked salmon on top and cut each slice in half. Set aside while you make the scrambled eggs.

2 Lightly beat the eggs together and season with salt and freshly ground black pepper. Melt the remaining butter in a pan until it is sizzling, then quickly pour in the beaten eggs stirring vigorously with a wooden spoon all the time. Do not let the eggs burn.

3 Stir constantly until the eggs begin to thicken. Just before they have finished cooking, stir in the cream.

4 Remove the pan from the heat and stir in the crème fraîche, add more salt and ground black pepper to taste.

5 Spoon the scrambled eggs on to the smoked salmon and bread on each plate. Top each serving with a spoonful of lumpfish roe or the salmon caviar and garnish with fresh sprigs of dill. Serve immediately.

Egg Crostini with Rouille

Crostini are extremely quick to make so are perfect for breakfast or brunch. The rouille gives them a hint of a Mediterranean flavour and provides the perfect complement to lightly fried eggs.

Serves 8

8 slices of ciabatta bread
extra virgin olive oil, for brushing
90ml/6 tbsp home-made mayonnaise
10ml/2 tsp harissa
8 eggs
8 small slices smoked ham
watercress or salad leaves, to serve

COOK'S TIP
Harissa is a fiery North African chilli paste made from dried red chillies, cumin, garlic, coriander, caraway and olive oil.

1 Preheat the oven to 200°C/400°F/ Gas 6. Use a pastry brush to lightly brush each slice of ciabatta bread with a little olive oil. Place the bread on a baking sheet and bake for 10 minutes, or until crisp and turning golden brown.

VARIATION
You can use 4 small portions of smoked haddock instead of ham and poach them for 5–7 minutes.

2 Meanwhile, make the rouille. Put the mayonnaise and harissa in a small bowl and mix well together.

3 Fry the eggs lightly in a little oil in a large non-stick frying pan.

4 Top the baked bread with the ham, eggs and a small spoonful of rouille. Serve immediately with watercress or salad leaves.

Polpettes

Little fried mouthfuls of potato and tangy-sharp Greek feta cheese, flavoured with dill and lemon juice, are ideal to serve for brunch or lunch.

Makes 12

500g/1¼lb floury potatoes
115g/4oz/1 cup feta cheese
4 spring onions (scallions), chopped
45ml/3 tbsp chopped fresh dill
1 egg, beaten
15ml/1 tbsp lemon juice
plain (all-purpose) flour, for dredging
45ml/3 tbsp olive oil
salt and ground black pepper
dill sprigs and shredded spring onions, to garnish
lemon wedges, to serve

1 Cook the potatoes in their skins in boiling lightly salted water until soft. Drain and leave to cool, then chop them in half and peel while still warm.

COOK'S TIP
To save time fry the polpettes in advance, cool and chill until required. Reheat in the oven before serving.

2 Place the potatoes in a bowl and mash until smooth. Crumble the feta cheese into the potatoes and add the spring onions, dill, egg and lemon juice and season with salt and pepper. (The cheese is salty, so taste before you add salt.) Stir well, until combined.

3 Cover and chill until firm. Divide the mixture into walnut-size balls, then flatten them slightly. Dredge with flour, shaking off the excess.

4 Heat the oil in a large frying pan and fry the polpettes in batches until golden brown on both sides. Drain on kitchen paper and serve hot, garnished with spring onions and sprigs of dill, and serve with lemon wedges.

Cheese and Leek Sausages with Chilli and Tomato Sauce

These popular vegetarian sausages, flavoured with herbs and served with a spicy sauce spiked with chilli and balsamic vinegar, are bound to be a hit for an informal lunch.

Makes 12

25g/1oz/2 tbsp butter
175g/6oz leeks, finely chopped
90ml/6 tbsp cold mashed potato
115g/4oz/2 cups fresh white
  breadcrumbs
150g/5oz/1¼ cups grated Caerphilly,
  Cheddar or Cantal cheese
30ml/2 tbsp chopped fresh parsley
5ml/1 tsp chopped fresh sage or
  marjoram
2 large (US extra large) eggs, beaten
good pinch of cayenne pepper
65g/2½oz/1 cup dry white
  breadcrumbs
oil, for shallow frying
salt and ground black pepper

For the sauce
30ml/2 tbsp olive oil
2 garlic cloves, thinly sliced
1 fresh red chilli, seeded and finely
  chopped, or a good pinch of dried
  red chilli flakes
1 small onion, finely chopped
500g/1¼lb tomatoes, peeled,
  seeded and chopped
a few fresh thyme sprigs
10ml/2 tsp balsamic vinegar or red
  wine vinegar
pinch of light muscovado
  (brown) sugar
15–30ml/1–2 tbsp chopped fresh
  marjoram or oregano

COOK'S TIP
These sausages are also delicious when they are served with a fruity chilli salsa and a watercress salad.

1 Melt the butter in a frying pan and fry the leeks for 4–5 minutes, or until softened but not browned. Mix with the mashed potato, fresh breadcrumbs, grated cheese, chopped parsley and sage or marjoram.

2 Add sufficient beaten egg (about two-thirds of the quantity) to bind the mixture together. Season well and add the cayenne pepper to taste.

3 Pat or roll the mixture between dampened hands to form 12 sausage shapes. Dip in the remaining egg, then coat in the dry breadcrumbs. Chill the coated sausages.

4 Make the sauce. Heat the oil in a pan and cook the garlic, chilli and onion over a low heat for 3–4 minutes. Add the tomatoes, thyme and vinegar. Season with salt, pepper and sugar.

5 Cook the sauce for 40–50 minutes, or until considerably reduced. Remove the thyme and purée the sauce in a food processor or blender. Reheat with the marjoram or oregano and then adjust the seasoning.

6 Fry the sausages in shallow oil until golden brown on all sides. Drain on kitchen paper and serve with the sauce.

Leek Roulade with Cheese, Walnut and Sweet Pepper Filling

This roulade is easy to prepare and is ideal for a vegetarian brunch, served with home-made tomato sauce.

Serves 6

butter or oil, for greasing
30ml/2 tbsp dry white breadcrumbs
75g/3oz/1 cup grated Parmesan cheese
50g/2oz/¼ cup butter
2 leeks, thinly sliced
40g/1½oz/⅓ cup plain
  (all-purpose) flour
250ml/8fl oz/1 cup milk
5ml/1 tsp Dijon mustard
1.5ml/¼ tsp freshly grated nutmeg
2 large (US extra large) eggs,
  separated, plus 1 egg white
2.5ml/½ tsp cream of tartar
salt and ground black pepper
rocket (arugula) and balsamic dressing,
  to serve

For the filling
2 large red (bell) peppers
350g/12oz/1½ cups ricotta cheese,
  curd cheese or soft goat's cheese
90g/3½oz/scant 1 cup chopped walnuts
4 spring onions (scallions), chopped
15g/½oz fresh basil leaves

1 Grease and line a 30 x 23cm/12 x 9in Swiss roll tin (jelly roll pan) with baking parchment, then sprinkle with the breadcrumbs and 30ml/2 tbsp of the grated Parmesan. Preheat the oven to 190°C/375°F/Gas 5.

2 Melt the butter in a pan and fry the leeks for 5 minutes, until softened.

3 Stir in the flour and cook over a low heat, stirring constantly, for 2 minutes, then gradually stir in the milk. Cook for 3–4 minutes, stirring constantly to make a thick sauce.

4 Stir in the mustard and nutmeg and season with salt and plenty of pepper. Reserve 30–45ml/2–3 tbsp of the remaining Parmesan, then stir the rest into the sauce. Cool slightly.

5 Beat the egg yolks into the sauce. In a clean bowl, whisk the egg whites and cream of tartar until stiff. Stir 2–3 spoonfuls of the egg white into the leek mixture, then carefully fold in the remaining egg white.

6 Pour the mixture into the tin and gently level it out using a spatula. Bake for 15–18 minutes, until risen and just firm to a light touch in the centre. If the roulade is to be served hot, increase the oven temperature to 200°C/400°F/ Gas 6 after removing the roulade.

7 Heat the grill (broiler). Halve and seed the peppers, grill (broil) them, skin sides uppermost, until black. Place in a bowl, cover and leave for 10 minutes. Peel and cut the flesh into strips. Mix the cheese, nuts and spring onions. Chop half the basil and stir into the mix.

8 Sprinkle the remaining Parmesan on to a large sheet of baking parchment. Turn out the roulade on to it. Strip off the lining paper and allow the roulade to cool. Spread the cheese mixture over it and top with the red pepper strips. Sprinkle the remaining basil leaves over the top. Roll up the roulade and place on to a platter. If serving hot, roll it on to a baking sheet, cover with a tent of foil and bake for 15–20 minutes. Serve with rocket and drizzle with dressing.

Potato and Red Pepper Frittata

For a light and easy-to-make lunch or a luxurious brunch with plenty of flavour and colour this frittata will certainly fit the bill. Serve it with a mixed salad to complement the crisp flavours of the fresh mint sprigs and red peppers. You can also make this a day in advance to take to a picnic or serve at a barbecue.

Serves 6 to 8

900g/2lb small new or salad potatoes
12 eggs
60ml/4 tbsp chopped fresh mint
60ml/4 tbsp olive oil
2 onions, chopped
4 garlic cloves, crushed
4 red (bell) peppers, seeded and
  roughly chopped
salt and ground black pepper
mint sprigs and crisp bacon, to garnish

1 Cook the potatoes in their skins in a large pan of lightly salted boiling water until they are just tender. Drain and leave to cool slightly, then cut the potaotes into thick slices.

2 Whisk together half the eggs, mint and seasoning in a large bowl, then set aside. Heat 30ml/2 tbsp oil in a large frying pan that can be safely used under the grill (broiler).

3 Add half the onion, garlic, peppers and potatoes to the pan and cook, stirring occasionally, for 5 minutes.

4 Pour the egg mixture into the frying pan and stir gently. Gently push the mixture towards the centre of the pan as it cooks to allow the liquid egg to run on to the base and cook through completely. Meanwhile, preheat the grill.

5 When the frittata is lightly set, place the pan under the hot grill for 2–3 minutes, or until the top is a light golden brown colour.

6 Make another frittata with the other half of the ingredients.

7 Serve hot or cold, cut into wedges piled high on a serving dish and garnished with mint and crisp bacon.

VARIATIONS
Lightly cooked broccoli florets, cut quite small, are delicious with or instead of peppers in this frittata. Roughly chopped black olives also go well with both peppers and broccoli.

Smoked Fish and Asparagus Mousse

This elegant mousse looks good with its studding of asparagus and smoked salmon. Serve a mustard and dill dressing separately if you like.

Serves 8

15ml/1 tbsp powdered gelatine
juice of 1 lemon
105ml/7 tbsp fish stock
50g/2oz/¼ cup butter, plus extra
    for greasing
2 shallots, finely chopped
225g/8oz smoked trout fillets
105ml/7 tbsp sour cream
225g/8oz/1 cup cream cheese or
    cottage cheese
1 egg white
12 spinach leaves, blanched
12 fresh asparagus spears,
    lightly cooked
115g/4oz smoked salmon, in strips
salt
shredded beetroot (beet) and beetroot
    leaves, to garnish

1 Sprinkle the gelatine over the lemon juice and leave until spongy. In a small pan, heat the fish stock, then add the soaked gelatine and stir to dissolve completely. Set aside. Melt the butter in a pan, add the shallots and cook gently until softened but not coloured.

2 Break up the smoked trout fillets and put them in a food processor with the shallots, sour cream, stock mixture and cream or cottage cheese. Whizz until smooth, then spoon into a bowl.

3 In a clean bowl, beat the egg white with a pinch of salt to soft peaks. Fold into the fish. Cover the bowl; chill for 30 minutes, or until starting to set.

4 Grease a 1 litre/1¾ pint/4 cup loaf tin (pan) or terrine with butter, then line it with the spinach leaves. Carefully spread half the trout mousse over the spinach-covered base, arrange the asparagus spears on top, then cover with the remaining trout mousse.

5 Arrange the smoked salmon strips lengthways on the mousse and fold over the overhanging spinach leaves. Cover with clear film (plastic wrap) and chill for 4 hours, until set. To serve, remove the clear film, turn out on to a serving dish and garnish with the shredded beetroot and leaves.

COOK'S TIP
Use a serrated knife with a fine-toothed blade to cut the mousse into neat slices.

Leek, Saffron and Mussel Tartlets

Serve these vividly coloured little tarts with cherry tomatoes and a few salad leaves, such as different lettuces or baby spinach.

Makes 12

4 large yellow (bell) peppers, halved
*   and seeded*
2kg/4½lb mussels, scrubbed and
*   beards removed*
large pinch of saffron threads
*   (about 30 strands)*
30ml/2 tbsp hot water
4 large leeks, sliced
60ml/4 tbsp olive oil
4 large (US extra large) eggs
600ml/1 pint/2½ cups single
*   (light) cream*
60ml/4 tbsp finely chopped
*   fresh parsley*
salt and ground black pepper
salad leaves, to serve

For the pastry
450g/1lb/4 cups plain
*   (all-purpose) flour*
5ml/1 tsp salt
250g/8oz/1 cup butter, diced
30–45ml/2–3 tbsp water

1 To make the pastry, mix together the flour, salt and butter. Using your fingertips to rub the butter into the flour until the mixture resembles fine breadcrumbs. Mix in the water and knead lightly to form a firm dough. Wrap the dough in clear film (plastic wrap) and chill for 30 minutes.

2 Grill (broil) the pepper halves, skin sides uppermost, until they are black. Place the peppers in a bowl, cover and leave for 10 minutes. When they are cool enough to handle, peel and cut the flesh into thin strips.

3 Scrub the mussel shells with a brush and rinse in cold running water.

4 Preheat the oven to 190°C/375°F/ Gas 5. Roll out the pastry and use it to line 12 x 10cm/4in tartlet tins, 2.5cm/ 1in deep. Prick the bases and then line the sides with strips of aluminium foil. Bake the pastry cases for 10 minutes. Remove the foil and bake for another 5–8 minutes, or until they are lightly coloured. Remove them from the oven. Reduce the oven temperature to 180°C/350°F/Gas 4.

5 Soak the saffron in the hot water for 10 minutes. Fry the leeks in the oil over a medium heat for 6–8 minutes until beginning to brown. Add the pepper strips and cook for another 2 minutes.

6 Bring 2.5cm/1in depth of water to a rolling boil in a large pan and add 10ml/2 tsp salt. Discard any open mussels that do not shut when tapped sharply, then throw the rest into the pan. Cover and cook over a high heat, shaking the pan occasionally, for 3–4 minutes, or until the mussels open. Discard any mussels that do not open. Shell the remainder.

7 Beat the eggs, cream and saffron liquid together. Season and whisk in the parsley. Arrange the leeks, peppers and mussels in the pastry, add the egg mixture and bake for 20–25 minutes, until just firm. Serve with salad leaves.

Roasted Vegetable and Garlic Sausage Loaf

Stuffed with cured meat and roasted vegetables, this crusty cob loaf makes a colourful centrepiece for a casual summer lunch or picnic. Serve with fresh green salad leaves.

Serves 6

1 large cob loaf
2 red (bell) peppers, quartered
  and seeded
1 large leek, sliced
90ml/6 tbsp olive oil
175g/6oz green beans, blanched
  and drained
75g/3oz garlic sausage, sliced
2 eggs, hard-boiled and quartered
115g/4oz/1 cup cashew nuts, toasted
75g/3oz/⅓ cup soft white (farmer's)
  cheese with garlic and herbs
salt and ground black pepper

1 Preheat the oven to 220°C/425°F/ Gas 7. Slice the top off the loaf using a large serrated knife and set it aside, then cut out the soft centre, leaving the crust intact. Stand the crusty shell on a baking sheet.

COOK'S TIP
Do not throw away the soft centre of the loaf. It can be made into breadcrumbs and frozen for use in another recipe.

2 Put the red peppers and sliced leek in a roasting pan with the olive oil and cook for 25–30 minutes, turning occasionally, or until the peppers have softened.

3 Spoon half of the pepper and leek mixture into the bottom of the loaf shell, pressing it down well with the back of a spoon. Add the green beans, garlic sausage, eggs and cashew nuts, packing the layers down well. Season each layer with salt and ground black pepper before adding the next. Dot the soft cheese with garlic and herbs over the filling and top with the remaining pepper and leek mixture.

4 Replace the top of the loaf and bake it for 15–20 minutes, or until the filling is warmed through. Serve, cut into wedges or slices.

VARIATION
You can use a variety of different-shaped loaves, such as a large, uncut white or wholemeal (whole-wheat) sandwich loaf, for this recipe. Hollow out the loaf and fill as above, then cut into slices.

Quiche Lorraine

This classic quiche from eastern France is perfect to serve at a relaxed lunch party. This recipe retains the traditional characteristics that are often forgotten in modern versions, namely very thin pastry, a really creamy and light, egg-rich filling and smoked bacon.

Serves 6 to 8

175g/6oz/1½ cups plain (all-purpose) flour, sifted
pinch of salt
115g/4oz/½ cup unsalted (sweet) butter, at room temperature, diced
3 eggs, plus 3 yolks
6 smoked streaky (fatty) bacon rashers (strips), rinds removed
300ml/½ pint/1¼ cups double (heavy) cream
25g/1oz/2 tbsp unsalted (sweet) butter
salt and ground black pepper

1 Place the flour, salt, butter and 1 egg yolk in a food processor and process until blended. Place on a floured surface and bring the mixture together into a ball. Leave to rest for 20 minutes.

2 Lightly flour a deep 20cm/8in round flan tin (quiche pan), and place it on a baking tray. Roll out the pastry and use to line the tin, trimming off any overhanging pieces. Press the pastry into the corners. If it breaks up, gently push it into shape. Chill for 20 minutes. Preheat the oven to 200°C/400°F/Gas 6.

3 Meanwhile, cut the bacon into thin strips and grill (broil) until the fat runs. Arrange the bacon in the pastry case. Beat together the cream, the remaining eggs and yolks and seasoning, and pour into the pastry case.

4 Bake for 15 minutes, then reduce the heat to 180°C/350°F/Gas 4 and bake for a further 15–20 minutes. When the filling is puffed up and golden brown and the pastry edge crisp, remove from the oven and top with pieces of butter. Leave for 5 minutes before serving.

Chicken Fajitas with Grilled Onions

Classic fajitas are fun to eat with friends and make a good choice for an informal lunch.

Serves 6

*finely grated rind of 1 lime and the
    juice of 2 limes*
120ml/4fl oz/½ cup olive oil
1 garlic clove, finely chopped
2.5ml/½ tsp dried oregano
good pinch of dried red chilli flakes
5ml/1 tsp coriander seeds, crushed
6 chicken breast fillets
3 Spanish onions, thickly sliced
*2 large red, yellow or orange (bell)
    peppers, seeded and cut into strips*
*30ml/2 tbsp chopped fresh
    coriander (cilantro)*
salt and ground black pepper

For the tomato salsa
*450g/1lb tomatoes, peeled, seeded
    and chopped*
2 garlic cloves, finely chopped
1 small red onion, finely chopped
1–2 green chillies, seeded and chopped
finely grated rind of ½ lime
*30ml/2 tbsp chopped fresh coriander
    (cilantro)*
pinch of caster (superfine) sugar
*2.5–5ml/½–1 tsp ground roasted
    cumin seeds*

To serve
12–18 soft flour tortillas
guacamole
120ml/4fl oz/½ cup sour cream
crisp lettuce leaves
coriander sprigs and lime wedges

1 In an ovenproof dish, combine the lime rind and juice, 75ml/5 tbsp of the oil, the garlic, oregano, chilli flakes and coriander seeds and season. Slash the skin on the chicken breast fillets several times and turn them in the mixture, then cover and set aside to marinate for several hours.

2 To make the salsa, combine the tomatoes, garlic, onion, chillies, lime rind and chopped coriander. Season to taste with salt, pepper, caster sugar and cumin seeds. Set aside for 30 minutes, then taste and adjust the seasoning, adding more cumin and sugar, if necessary.

3 Heat the grill (broiler). Thread the onion slices on to a skewer or place them on a grill rack. Brush with 15ml/ 1 tbsp of the remaining oil and season. Grill (broil) until softened and slightly charred in places. Preheat the oven to 200°C/400°F/Gas 6.

4 Cook the chicken breast fillets in their marinade, covered, in the oven for 20 minutes. Remove from the oven, then grill (broil) the chicken for 8–10 minutes, or until browned and fully cooked right through.

5 Meanwhile, heat the remaining oil in a large frying pan and cook the peppers for about 10 minutes, or until softened and browned in places. Add the grilled onions and fry for 2–3 minutes.

6 Add the chicken cooking juices and fry over a high heat, stirring frequently, until the liquid evaporates. Stir in the chopped coriander.

7 Reheat the tortillas following the instructions on the packet. Using a sharp knife, cut the grilled chicken into strips and transfer to a serving dish. Place the onion and pepper mixture and the salsa in separate dishes.

8 Serve the dishes of chicken, onions and peppers and salsa with the tortillas, guacamole, sour cream, lettuce and coriander for people to help themselves. Serve with lime wedges.

Turkey Croquettes

Smoked turkey gives these crisp croquettes a distinctive flavour. Served with the tangy tomato sauce, crispy bread and salad they make a tasty meal.

Makes 8

450g/1lb maincrop potatoes, diced
3 eggs
30ml/2 tbsp milk
175g/6oz smoked turkey rashers
*   (strips), finely chopped*
2 spring onions (scallions), finely sliced
115g/4oz/2 cups fresh white
*   breadcrumbs*
vegetable oil, for deep-frying
salt and ground black pepper

For the sauce
15ml/1 tbsp olive oil
1 onion, finely chopped
400g/14oz can tomatoes, drained
30ml/2 tbsp tomato purée (paste)
15ml/1 tbsp chopped fresh parsley

1 Boil the potatoes until tender. Drain and return the pan to a low heat to make sure all the excess water evaporates.

2 Mash the potatoes with two eggs and the milk. Season well with salt and pepper. Stir in the turkey rashers and spring onions. Chill for 1 hour.

3 To make the sauce, heat the oil in a frying pan and fry the onion until softened. Add the tomatoes and tomato purée, stir and simmer for 10 minutes. Stir in the parsley and season Keep the sauce warm until needed.

4 Remove the potato mixture from the refrigerator and divide into eight pieces. Shape each piece into a sausage and dip in the remaining beaten egg and then the breadcrumbs.

5 Heat the vegetable oil in a pan or deep-fryer to 190°C/375°F. Test this by dropping a cube of day-old bread into the hot oil, it should brown in 60 seconds. Deep-fry the croquettes for 5 minutes, or until they are golden and crisp. Reheat the sauce gently, if necessary, and serve with the freshly cooked croquettes.

informal suppers

Sharing a large dish is a sure way

of having a memorable no-fuss

meal with friends.

Tofu and Vegetable Thai Curry

Traditional Thai ingredients – chillies, galangal, lemon grass and kaffir lime leaves – give this vegetarian curry a wonderfully fragrant aroma. It makes an excellent main course when served with boiled jasmine rice or noodles.

Serves 8

350g/12oz tofu, drained
90ml/6 tbsp dark soy sauce
30ml/2 tbsp sesame oil
10ml/2 tsp chilli sauce
5cm/2in piece fresh root ginger,
   finely grated
450g/1lb cauliflower
450g/1lb broccoli
60ml/4 tbsp vegetable oil
2 onions, peeled and sliced
750ml/1¼ pints/3 cups coconut milk
300ml/½ pint/1¼ cups water
2 red (bell) peppers, seeded
   and chopped
350g/12oz green beans, halved
225g/8oz/3 cups shiitake or button
   (white) mushrooms, halved
shredded spring onions (scallions),
   to garnish
boiled jasmine rice or noodles,
   to serve

For the curry paste
4 chillies, seeded and chopped
2 lemon grass stalks, chopped
5cm/2in piece fresh galangal, chopped
4 kaffir lime leaves
20ml/4 tsp ground coriander
a few sprigs fresh coriander (cilantro),
   including the stalks

1 Cut the drained tofu into 2.5cm/1in cubes and place in an ovenproof dish. Mix together the soy sauce, sesame oil, chilli sauce and ginger and pour over the tofu. Toss gently then marinate for at least 2 hours or overnight, turning and basting the tofu occasionally.

2 To make the curry paste, blend the chopped chillies, lemon grass, galangal, kaffir lime leaves, ground and fresh coriander in a food processor for a few seconds. Add 90ml/6 tbsp water and process to a thick paste.

3 Preheat the oven to 190°C/375°F/Gas 5. Using a sharp knife cut the cauliflower and broccoli into florets and cut any stalks into thin slices.

4 Heat the vegetable oil in a frying pan, add the sliced onions and gently fry for about 8 minutes, or until soft and lightly browned. Stir in the prepared curry paste and the coconut milk. Add the water and bring to the boil.

5 Stir in the red peppers, green beans, cauliflower and broccoli. Transfer to a casserole. Cover and place in the oven.

6 Stir the tofu and marinade, then place the dish in the top of the oven and cook for 30 minutes. Add the marinade mixture and mushrooms to the curry. Reduce the oven temperature to 180°C/350°F/Gas 4 and cook for about 15 minutes, or until the vegetables are tender. Garnish the curry with shredded spring onions. Serve with boiled jasmine rice or noodles.

Swiss Cheese Fondue with Vegetables

This classic, richly flavoured fondue is traditionally served with cubes of bread, but here it is updated with herby vegetable dippers and toasted garlic croûtes.

Serves 4 to 6

2 French batons or 1 baguette
1–2 garlic cloves, halved
1 small head broccoli, divided
*   into florets*
1 small head cauliflower, divided
*   into florets*
200g/7oz mangetouts (snow peas)
*   or green beans, trimmed*
115g/4oz baby carrots, trimmed,
*   or 2 medium carrots, cut into wedges*
250ml/8fl oz/1 cup dry white wine
115g/4oz/1 cup grated Gruyère cheese
250ml/8fl oz/2¼ cups grated
*   Emmenthal cheese*
15ml/1tbsp cornflour (cornstarch)
30ml/2tbsp Kirsch
freshly grated nutmeg
salt and ground black pepper

For the dressing
30ml/2 tbsp extra virgin olive oil
rind and juice of 2 lemons
25g/1oz/½ cup chopped fresh parsley
25g/1oz/½ cup chopped fresh mint
1 red chilli, seeded and finely chopped

1 Cut the batons or baguette on the diagonal into 1cm/½in slices, then toast on both sides. Rub one side of each slice with the cut side of a garlic clove, if you like, and transfer to a platter.

2 Blanch all the vegetables for 2 minutes in a large pan of salted boiling water, then place them in a large bowl. While they are hot, add all the dressing ingredients, season, and toss together.

3 Rub the inside of the fondue pot with the cut side of a garlic clove. Pour in the white wine and heat gently on the stove. Gradually add the grated cheeses to the pot, stirring constantly until melted. Mix the cornflour with the Kirsch and add, then stir until thickened.

4 Season with salt, ground black pepper and grated nutmeg to taste. When the fondue is hot and smooth, but not boiling, transfer to a burner at the table.

5 Each diner dips the vegetables and toasted bread into the fondue.

VARIATIONS
• Use fresh chopped basil instead of mint.
• Use crunchy, fresh vegetables such as pink radishes, mushrooms, baby corn and red or yellow (bell) peppers.

Seafood Laksa

A laksa is a Malaysian stew of fish, poultry, meat or vegetables with noodles. Authentic laksas are often very hot, and cooled by coconut milk and the noodles. If you prefer a hot and spicy version, add a little chilli powder instead of some of the paprika.

Serves 8 to 10

4 medium-hot fresh red chillies, seeded
6–8 garlic cloves
10ml/2 tsp mild paprika
20ml/4 tsp fermented shrimp paste
45ml/3 tbsp chopped fresh root
  ginger or galangal
500g/1¼ lb small red shallots
50g/2oz fresh coriander (cilantro),
  preferably with roots
90ml/6 tbsp groundnut (peanut) oil
10ml/2 tsp fennel seeds, crushed
4 fennel bulbs, cut into thin wedges
1.2 litres/2 pints/5 cups fish stock
600g/1 lb 6oz thin vermicelli
  rice noodles
900ml/1½ pints/3¾ cups coconut milk
juice of 2–4 limes
60–90ml/4–6 tbsp Thai fish sauce
  (nam pla)
900g/2lb firm white fish fillet, such as
  monkfish, halibut or snapper
900g/2lb large raw prawns (shrimp)
  (about 40), shelled and deveined
bunch of fresh basil
4 spring onions (scallions),
  thinly sliced

1 Process the chillies, garlic, paprika, shrimp paste, ginger or galangal and four shallots to a paste in a food processor, blender or spice grinder. Remove the roots and stems from the coriander and add them to the paste; chop and reserve the coriander leaves. Add 30ml/2 tbsp of the groundnut oil to the paste and process again until fairly smooth.

2 Heat the remaining oil in a large pan or stockpot. Add the remaining shallots, the fennel seeds and fennel wedges. Cook until lightly browned, then add 90ml/6 tbsp of the paste and stir-fry for about 2 minutes. Pour in the fish stock and bring to the boil. Reduce the heat and simmer for 8–10 minutes.

3 Meanwhile, cook the vermicelli rice noodles according to the instructions on the packet. Drain and set aside.

4 Pour the coconut milk into the pan of shallots, stirring continuously to prevent sticking, then add the juice of two limes, with 60ml/4 tbsp of the fish sauce. Stir well to combine. Bring to a simmer and taste, adding more of the curry paste, lime juice or fish sauce as necessary to taste.

5 Cut the fish into chunks and add to the pan. Cook for 3–4 minutes, then add the prawns and cook until they turn pink. Chop most of the basil and add to the pan with the reserved chopped coriander leaves.

6 Divide the noodles among 8–10 bowls, then ladle in the stew. Sprinkle with spring onions and the remaining whole basil leaves. Serve immediately.

Tempura

This flavourful Japanese dish of crunchy battered vegetables and crispy squid rings is served with a piquant dipping sauce. Tempura can be cooked at the table over a special spillproof spirit burner making it ideal for a party.

Serves 8 to 10

2 medium aubergines (eggplant)
4 red (bell) peppers, seeded
500g/1¼ lb/5 cups plain (all-purpose)
*   flour, plus extra for dusting*
8 baby squid, cut into rings
400g/14oz green beans, trimmed
24 mint sprigs
oil, for deep-frying
4 egg yolks
1 litre/1¾ pints/4 cups iced water
10ml/2 tsp salt
gari (Japanese pickled ginger) or grated
*   fresh root ginger, and grated daikon*
*   or pink radishes, to serve*

For the dipping sauce
400ml/14fl oz/1⅔ cups water
90ml/6 tbsp mirin or sweet sherry
20g/½oz bonito flakes (see Cook's Tip)
90ml/6 tbsp soy sauce

1 To make the dipping sauce, mix the sauce ingredients together in a pan, bring to the boil and then strain into serving saucers and leave to cool.

COOK'S TIP
If you cannot get hold of bonito flakes, an acceptable substitute would be to use 200ml/7fl oz/scant 1 cup fish stock instead of the water to make the dipping sauce.

VARIATIONS
• Any seafood is suitable for cooking in a tempura batter. Try mussels, clams, prawns (shrimp) or scallops, or slices of salmon, cod, tuna or haddock.
• Cauliflower, broccoli, and mangetouts (snow peas) work well, too.

2 Cut the aubergine and peppers into fine julienne strips using a sharp knife or a mandolin. Put the flour for dusting into a plastic bag and add the squid. Shake the bag to coat the squid with a little flour, then place on a serving dish. Repeat with the vegetables and mint.

3 Heat the oil for deep-frying in a wok or deep pan to 190°C/375°F. If you do not have a cook's thermometer, test by dropping a cube of day-old bread into the hot oil; it should brown in 30–60 seconds. Transfer to a burner at the table. Never leave it unattended.

4 When ready to eat, beat the egg yolks and the iced water together. Tip in the flour and salt, and stir briefly. It is important that the tempura is lumpy and not mixed to a smooth batter.

5 Each diner dips the food into the batter and then immediately into the hot oil using chopsticks, long fondue forks or wire baskets. Fry for 2 minutes, or until crisp.

6 Serve the tempura dipped in the sauce and accompanied by gari or ginger and daikon or radishes.

Celebration Paella

This paella is a marvellous mixture of some of the finest Spanish ingredients and makes a colourful one-pot party dish.

Serves 6 to 8

6–8 large raw prawns (shrimp), peeled,
or 12–16 smaller raw prawns
450g/1lb fresh mussels
90ml/6 tbsp white wine
150g/5oz green beans, cut into
2.5cm/1in lengths
115g/4oz/1 cup frozen broad
(fava) beans
6 small skinless chicken breast fillets,
cut into large pieces
30ml/2 tbsp plain (all-purpose) flour,
seasoned with salt and pepper
about 90ml/6 tbsp olive oil
150g/5oz pork fillet, cut into
bitesize pieces
2 onions, chopped
2–3 garlic cloves, crushed
1 red (bell) pepper, seeded and sliced
2 ripe tomatoes, peeled, seeded
and chopped
900ml/1½ pints/3¾ cups well-
flavoured chicken stock
good pinch of saffron threads,
dissolved in 30ml/2 tbsp hot water
350g/12oz/1¾ cups Spanish rice or
risotto rice
225g/8oz chorizo, sliced
115g/4oz/1 cup frozen peas
6–8 stuffed green olives,
thickly sliced
salt and ground black pepper

COOK'S TIP
Ideally, you should use a paella pan for this recipe and the paella should not be stirred during cooking. However, you may find that the rice cooks in the centre but not around the outside. To make sure it cooks evenly stir occasionally, or cook the paella on the bottom of a hot 190°C/375°F/Gas 5 oven for about 15–18 minutes.

1 Make a shallow cut down the centre of the curved back of each of the large prawns. Pull out the black veins with a cocktail stick (toothpick) or your fingers, then rinse the prawns thoroughly and set them aside.

2 Scrub the mussels' shells with a stiff brush and rinse thoroughly under cold running water. Scrape off any barnacles and remove the "beards" with a small knife. Rinse well. Discard any mussels that are open and do not close when sharply tapped.

3 Place the mussels in a large pan with the wine, bring to the boil, then cover the pan tightly and cook for 3–4 minutes, or until the mussels have opened, shaking the pan occasionally. Drain, reserving the liquid and discarding any mussels that remain closed.

4 Briefly cook the green beans and broad beans in separate pans of boiling water for 2–3 minutes. Drain. As soon as the broad beans are cool enough to handle, pop the bright green inner beans out of their skins.

5 Dust the chicken with the seasoned flour. Heat half the oil in a paella pan or frying pan and fry the chicken until browned all over. Transfer to a plate. Next, fry the prawns briefly, adding more oil if needed, use a slotted spoon to transfer them to a plate. Heat a further 30ml/2 tbsp of the oil in the pan and brown the pork. Transfer to a plate.

6 Heat the remaining oil and fry the onions and garlic for 3–4 minutes, or until golden brown. Add the red pepper, cook for 2–3 minutes, then add the chopped tomatoes and cook until the mixture is fairly thick.

7 Stir in the chicken stock, the reserved mussel liquid and the saffron liquid. Season well with salt and pepper and bring to the boil. When the liquid is bubbling, add the rice. Stir once, then add the chicken pieces, pork, prawns, beans, chorizo and peas. Cook over a moderately high heat for 12 minutes, then lower the heat and leave to cook for 8–10 minutes more, until all the liquid has been absorbed.

8 Add the mussels and olives and continue cooking for a further 3–4 minutes to heat through. Remove the pan from the heat, cover with a clean damp dishtowel and leave the paella to stand for 10 minutes before serving from the pan.

Mongolian Firepot

Cooking at the table in a firepot is a fun and sociable way to enjoy a meal with family or friends. It calls for plenty of participation on the part of the guests, who cook the assembled ingredients, dipping the meats in a variety of different sauces.

Serves 6 to 8

900g/2lb boned leg of lamb, preferably bought thinly sliced
225g/8oz lamb's liver and/or kidneys
900ml/1½ pints/3¾ cups lamb stock (see Cook's Tip)
900ml/1½ pints/3¾ cups chicken stock
1cm/½ in piece fresh root ginger, peeled and thinly sliced
45ml/3 tbsp rice wine or medium-dry sherry
½ head Chinese leaves (Chinese cabbage), rinsed and shredded
few young spinach leaves
250g/9oz fresh firm tofu, diced (optional)
115g/4oz cellophane noodles
salt and ground black pepper

For the dipping sauce
50ml/2fl oz/¼ cup red wine vinegar
7.5ml/1½ tsp dark soy sauce
1cm/½ in piece fresh root ginger, peeled and finely shredded
1 spring onion (scallion), shredded

To serve
bowls of tomato sauce, sweet chilli sauce, mustard oil and sesame oil
dry-fried coriander seeds, crushed

COOK'S TIP
To make lamb stock, place the leg bones in a large pan with water to cover. Bring to the boil and skim the surface. Add 1 peeled onion, 2 carrots, 1cm/½ in piece of peeled and bruised ginger, 5ml/1 tsp salt and ground black pepper. Bring back to the boil, then simmer for about 1 hour. Strain, cool, then skim and use.

1 When buying the lamb, ask your butcher to slice it thinly on a slicing machine, if possible. If you have had to buy the lamb in one piece, however, put it in the freezer for about an hour, so that it is easier to slice thinly.

2 Trim the liver and remove the skin and core from the kidneys, if using. Place them in the freezer, too. If you managed to buy sliced lamb, keep it in the refrigerator until needed.

3 Mix both types of stock in a large pan. Add the sliced ginger and rice wine or sherry, with salt and pepper to taste. Heat to simmering point; simmer for 15 minutes.

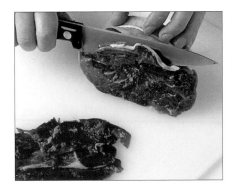

4 Slice all the meats thinly and arrange them attractively on a large platter.

5 Place the shredded Chinese leaves, spinach leaves and the diced tofu on a separate platter.

6 Soak the noodles in warm or hot water, following the instructions given on the packet.

7 Make the dipping sauce by mixing all the ingredients in a small bowl. The other sauces and the crushed coriander seeds should be spooned into separate small dishes and placed on a serving tray or on the table.

8 When you are ready to eat, set the firepot on the dining table and light the burner. Fill the moat of the hotpot with the simmering stock. Alternatively, fill a fondue pot and place it over a burner. Remember never to leave the lighted burner unattended. Each guest selects a portion of meat from the platter and cooks it in the hot stock, using chopsticks, a little wire basket (usually sold alongside firepots) or a fondue fork. The meat is then dipped in one of the sauces and coated with the coriander seeds (if you like).

9 When most of the meat has been eaten, top up the stock if necessary, then add the vegetables, tofu and drained noodles. Cook until the noodles are tender and the vegetables retain a little crispness. Serve the soup in warmed bowls.

Beef Carbonade

This rich, dark stew of beef, cooked slowly with lots of onions, garlic and beer, is a classic one-pot casserole from the north of France and Belgium. Serve with roasted potatoes, if you like.

Serves 6

45ml/3 tbsp vegetable oil or
  beef dripping
3 onions, sliced
45ml/3 tbsp plain (all-purpose) flour
2.5ml/½ tsp mustard powder
1kg/2¼lb stewing beef (shin or chuck),
  cut into large cubes
2–3 garlic cloves, finely chopped
300ml/½ pint/1¼ cups dark beer or ale
150ml/¼ pint/⅔ cup water
5ml/1 tsp soft dark brown sugar
1 fresh thyme sprig
1 fresh bay leaf
1 celery stick
salt and ground black pepper

For the topping
50g/2oz/½ cup butter
1 garlic clove, crushed
15ml/1 tbsp Dijon mustard
45ml/3 tbsp chopped fresh parsley
6–12 slices baguette or ficelle loaf

1 Preheat the oven to 160°C/325°F/ Gas 3. Heat 30ml/2 tbsp of the oil or dripping in a frying pan and cook the onions over a low heat until softened. Remove from the pan and set aside.

2 Meanwhile, mix together the flour and mustard and season. Toss the beef in the flour. Add the remaining oil or dripping to the pan and heat over a high heat. Brown the beef all over, then transfer it to a casserole dish.

COOK'S TIP
When making more than double the quantity, limit the garlic cloves to 8 in total, otherwise the flavour is too strong.

3 Reduce the heat and return the onions to the pan. Add the garlic, cook, then add the beer or ale, water and sugar. Tie the thyme and bay leaf together and add to the pan with the celery. Bring to the boil, stirring, then season.

4 Pour the sauce over the beef and mix. Cover, then place in the oven for 2½ hours. Check the beef, add more water if it seems too dry. Test for tenderness, and cook for 30–40 minutes more, if necessary.

5 To make the topping, cream the butter together with the garlic, mustard and 30ml/2 tbsp of the parsley. Spread the butter thickly over the bread.

6 Increase the oven temperature to 190°C/375°F/Gas 5. Taste and season the casserole, then arrange the bread slices, buttered side uppermost, on top. Bake for 20–25 minutes, until the bread is browned. Sprinkle the remaining parsley over the top and serve.

Moussaka

Layers of minced lamb, aubergines, tomatoes and onions are topped with a creamy yogurt and cheese sauce in this delicious, authentic eastern Mediterranean recipe. Serve with a simple, mixed leaf, green salad.

Serves 8

900g/2lb aubergines (eggplant)
300ml/½ pint/1⅓ cups olive oil
2 large onions, chopped
4–6 garlic cloves, finely chopped
1.3kg/3lb lean minced (ground) lamb
30ml/2 tbsp plain (all-purpose) flour
2 x 400g/14oz cans chopped tomatoes
60ml/4 tbsp chopped mixed fresh
herbs, such as parsley, marjoram
and oregano
salt and ground black pepper

For the topping
600ml/1 pint/2½ cups natural (plain)
yogurt
4 eggs
50g/2oz feta cheese, crumbled
50g/2oz/⅔ cup grated Parmesan cheese

1 Cut the aubergines into thin slices and layer them in a colander, sprinkling each layer with salt.

2 Cover the aubergines with a plate and a weight, then leave to drain for about 30 minutes. Drain and rinse well, then pat dry with kitchen paper.

3 Heat 90ml/6 tbsp of the olive oil in a large, heavy pan. Fry the chopped onion and garlic until softened, but not coloured. Add the lamb and cook over a high heat, stirring often, until lightly browned.

4 Stir in the flour until mixed, then stir in the tomatoes, herbs and seasoning. Bring to the boil, reduce the heat and simmer gently for 20 minutes.

5 Meanwhile, heat a little of the remaining oil in a large frying pan. Add as many aubergine slices as can be laid in the pan, then cook until golden on both sides. Set the cooked aubergines aside. Heat more oil and continue frying the aubergines in batches, adding oil as necessary.

6 Preheat the oven to 180°C/350°F/ Gas 4. Arrange half the aubergine slices in a large, shallow ovenproof dish or divide among two smaller dishes.

7 Top the aubergine slices with about half of the meat and tomato mixture, then add the remaining aubergine slices. Spread the remaining meat mixture over the aubergines.

8 Beat together the yogurt and eggs, mix in the feta and Parmesan cheeses, and spread the mixture over the meat.

9 Transfer the moussaka to the oven and bake for 35–40 minutes, or until golden and bubbling.

Red Chicken Curry with Bamboo Shoots

Bamboo shoots have a lovely crunchy texture and make a delightful, contrasting texture to the chicken in this Thai curry. It is perfect served with jasmine rice.

Serves 6

1 litre/1¾ pints/4 cups coconut milk
30ml/2 tbsp red curry paste
450g/1lb chicken breast fillets, skinned and cut into bitesize pieces
30ml/2 tbsp Thai fish sauce (nam pla)
15ml/1 tbsp sugar
225g/8oz canned whole bamboo shoots, rinsed, drained and sliced
5 kaffir lime leaves, torn
salt and ground black pepper
chopped fresh red chillies and kaffir lime leaves, to garnish

For the red curry paste
5ml/1tsp roasted coriander seeds
2.5ml/½ tsp roasted cumin seeds
6–8 fresh red chillies, seeded and chopped
4 shallots, thinly sliced
2 garlic cloves, peeled and chopped
15ml/1 tbsp fresh galangal, peeled and chopped
2 lemon grass stalks, chopped
4 fresh coriander (cilantro) roots
10 black peppercorns
pinch of ground cinnamon
5ml/1 tsp ground turmeric
2.5ml/½ tsp shrimp paste
5ml/1 tsp salt
30 ml/2 tbsp vegetable oil

1 To make the red curry paste, put all the ingredients except the oil into a mortar or food processor and pound or process to a paste. Add the oil a little at a time, mixing or processing well after each addition. If you are not using the paste immediately, transfer it to a jar, and keep in the refrigerator until you are ready to use it. For a hotter paste, add a few chilli seeds.

2 Pour half of the coconut milk into a wok or large pan over a medium heat. Bring to the boil, stirring constantly, with large cooking chopsticks or a spoon until it has separated.

3 Add the red curry paste and cook the mixture for 2–3 minutes. Stir the paste constantly to prevent it from sticking to the base of the pan.

4 Add the chicken pieces, fish sauce and sugar to the pan. Stir well, then cook for 5–6 minutes, or until the chicken changes colour and is cooked through. Continue to stir during cooking to prevent the mixture from sticking to the base of the pan and to ensure that the chicken cooks evenly.

5 Pour the remaining coconut milk into the pan, then add the sliced bamboo shoots and torn kaffir lime leaves. Bring back to the boil over a medium heat, stirring constantly to prevent the mixture from sticking, then taste and add salt and pepper if necessary.

6 To serve, spoon the curry into a warmed serving dish and garnish with chopped chillies and kaffir lime leaves.

COOK'S TIP
Preparing a double or larger quantity of paste in a food processor or blender makes the blending of the ingredients easier and the paste will be smoother. Store surplus curry paste in the freezer.

VARIATIONS
• For green curry paste, process 12–15 green chillies, 2 chopped lemon grass stalks, 3 sliced shallots, 2 garlic cloves, 15ml/1 tbsp chopped galangal, 4 chopped kaffir lime leaves, 2.5ml/½ tsp grated kaffir rind, 5ml/1 tsp each of chopped coriander root, salt, roasted coriander seeds, roasted cumin seeds and shrimp paste, 15ml/1 tbsp sugar, 6 black peppercorns and 15ml/1 tbsp vegetable oil until a paste forms.
• For yellow curry paste, process 6–8 yellow chillies, 1 chopped lemon grass stalk, 2 sliced shallots, 4 garlic cloves, 15ml/1 tbsp chopped fresh root ginger, 5ml/1 tsp ground cinnamon,15ml/1 tbsp light brown sugar and 30ml/2 tbsp vegetable oil until a paste forms.
• Use turkey or pork instead of chicken.

dinner party soups and appetizers

These tempting first courses are all visually appealing and perfect for setting the right tone at the beginning of a special meal.

Vichyssoise with Watercress Cream

Classic soups, such as this cold French version of leek and potato soup, will always remain firm favourites for dinner parties.

Serves 6

50g/2oz/¼ cup butter
1 onion, sliced
450g/1lb leeks, sliced
225g/8oz potatoes, sliced
750ml/1¼ pints/3 cups chicken stock
300ml/½ pint/1¼ cups milk
45ml/3 tbsp single (light) cream
salt and ground black pepper
fresh parsley, to garnish

For the watercress cream
1 bunch watercress, about 75g/3oz,
    stalks removed
small bunch of fresh chervil,
    finely chopped
150ml/¼ pint/⅔ cup double
    (heavy) cream
pinch of freshly grated nutmeg

1 Melt the butter in a pan. Add the onion and leeks, cover and cook gently for 10 minutes, stirring occasionally, until softened. Stir in the potatoes and stock, and bring to the boil. Reduce the heat and simmer for 20 minutes, or until the potatoes are tender. Cool slightly.

2 Process the soup in a food processor or blender until smooth, then press through a sieve into a clean pan.

3 Stir in the milk and single cream. Season the soup well and chill for at least 2 hours.

4 To make the watercress cream, process the watercress in a food processor or blender until finely chopped, then stir in the chervil and cream. Pour into a bowl and stir in the nutmeg with seasoning to taste.

5 Ladle the soup into bowls and spoon the watercress cream on top. Garnish with parsley and serve.

COOK'S TIP
The soup is also delicious served hot in winter, especially sprinkled with a little grated nutmeg.

Iced Melon Soup with Melon and Mint Sorbet

You can use different melons for the cool soup and ice sorbet to create a subtle contrast in flavour and colour. Try a combination of Charentais and Ogen or cantaloupe and Galia. This soup is refreshing and ideal for formal and informal summer dinner parties, and *al fresco* dining.

Serves 6 to 8

2.25kg/5lb very ripe melon
45ml/3 tbsp orange juice
30ml/2 tbsp lemon juice
mint leaves, to garnish

For the melon and mint sorbet
25g/1oz/2 tbsp sugar
120ml/4fl oz/½ cup water
2.25kg/5lb very ripe melon
juice of 2 limes
30ml/2 tbsp chopped fresh mint

1 To make the melon and mint sorbet, put the sugar and water into a pan and heat gently until the sugar dissolves. Bring to the boil and simmer for 4–5 minutes, then leave to cool.

2 Halve the melon. Scrape out the seeds, then cut it into large wedges and cut the flesh out of the skin. It should weigh about 1.6kg/3½lb.

3 Purée the melon flesh in a food processor or blender with the cooled syrup and lime juice.

4 If you are using an ice cream maker: stir in the mint and pour in the melon mixture. Churn, following the maker's instructions, or until the sorbet is smooth and firm. By hand: stir in the mint and pour the mixture into a freezer-proof container. Freeze until icy at the edges. Transfer to a food processor and process until smooth. Repeat this process until the mixture is smooth and holding its shape, then freeze until firm.

5 To make the chilled melon soup, prepare the melon as in step 2 and purée until smooth in a food processor or blender. Pour the purée into a bowl and stir in the orange and lemon juice. Place the soup in the refrigerator for 30–40 minutes, but do not chill it for too long as this will dull its flavour.

6 Ladle the soup into bowls and add a large scoop of the melon and mint sorbet to each. Garnish with mint leaves and serve immediately.

COOK'S TIP

The soup also looks impressive served in large wine glasses, with small balls of sorbet instead of large scoops. Keep the glasses cool by standing them in bowls filled with ice cubes.

Cream of Mushroom Soup with Goat's Cheese Crostini

Classic cream of mushroom soup is still a firm favourite, especially with the addition of crisp and garlicky croûtes with tangy goat's cheese.

Serves 6

25g/1oz/2 tbsp butter
1 onion, chopped
1 garlic clove, chopped
450g/1lb/6 cups chestnut or brown cap (cremini) mushrooms, some whole, some roughly chopped
15ml/1 tbsp plain (all-purpose) flour
45ml/3 tbsp dry sherry
900ml/1½ pints/3¾ cups vegetable stock
150ml/¼ pint/⅔ cup double (heavy) cream
salt and ground black pepper
fresh parsley sprigs, to garnish

For the crostini
15ml/1 tbsp olive oil, plus extra for brushing
1 shallot, chopped
115g/4oz/2 cups button (white) mushrooms, finely chopped
15ml/1 tbsp chopped fresh parsley
6 brown cap (cremini) mushrooms
6 slices baguette
1 small garlic clove
115g/4oz/1 cup soft goat's cheese

1 Melt the butter, cook the onion and garlic for 5 minutes. Add the mushrooms, cover, cook for 10 minutes.

2 Stir in the flour and cook for 1 minute. Stir in the dry sherry and stock and bring to the boil, then simmer for 15 minutes. Cool slightly, then purée the mixture in a food processor or blender until smooth.

3 Meanwhile, prepare the crostini. Heat the oil in a small pan. Add the shallot and button mushrooms, and cook for 8–10 minutes, until softened. Drain well and transfer to a food processor or blender. Add the fresh parsley and process the mushroom mixture until finely chopped.

4 Preheat the grill (broiler). Brush the brown cap mushrooms with oil and grill (broil) for 5–6 minutes.

5 Toast the slices of baguette, rub with the garlic and put a spoonful of cheese on each. Top the grilled mushrooms with the mushroom mixture and place on the crostini.

6 Return the soup to the pan and stir in the cream. Season, then reheat gently. Ladle the soup into six bowls. Float a crostini in the centre of each and garnish with chervil.

Cappuccino of **Puy Lentils, Lobster** and **Tarragon**

Here is a really impressive soup to start a dinner party with. Adding ice-cold butter a little at a time is the secret of whipping up the good froth that gives the soup its clever cappuccino effect.

Serves 6

450–675g/1–1½ lb live lobster
150g/5oz/⅔ cup Puy lentils
1 carrot, halved
1 celery stick, halved
1 small onion, halved
1 garlic clove
1 bay leaf
large bunch of tarragon, tied firmly
1 litre/1¾ pints/4 cups fish stock
120ml/4fl oz/½ cup double
    (heavy) cream
25g/1oz/2 tbsp butter, finely diced and
    chilled until ice cold
salt and ground black pepper
fresh tarragon sprigs, to garnish

1 Lower the live lobster into a large stockpot of water. Cover the pan and bring to the boil. Cook for 15–20 minutes, then drain the lobster and leave to cool.

2 Put the Puy lentils in a large pan and pour in enough cold water to cover. Add the carrot, celery, onion, garlic and herbs. Bring the water to the boil and simmer for 20 minutes.

3 Drain the lentils and discard the herbs and vegetables. Purée the lentils in a food processor until smooth. Set aside.

4 Break the claws off the lobster, crack them open and remove all the meat from inside. Break off the tail, split it open and remove the meat. Cut all the meat into bitesize pieces.

5 Pour the fish stock into a large clean pan and bring to the boil. Lightly stir in the lentil purée and cream, but do not mix too much at this point otherwise you will not be able to create the frothy effect. The mixture should still be quite watery in places. Season well.

6 Using either a hand-held blender or electric beater, whisk up the soup mixture, adding the butter one piece at a time, until it is very frothy.

7 Divide the lobster meat among the bowls and carefully pour in the soup. Garnish with sprigs of tarragon and serve immediately.

COOK'S TIP

Instead of adding the live lobster to the pan, kill it first by freezing it overnight. Cook from frozen, allowing 30 minutes in the boiling water. The other way of killing lobster is by stabbing it in the back of the head, where the tail shell meets the head.

Pancakes with Leek, Chicory and Squash Stuffing

Serve a chunky home-made tomato sauce and a crisp salad with these melt-in-the-mouth stuffed pancakes.

Serves 8

225g/8oz/2 cups plain
(all-purpose) flour
115g/4oz/1 cup yellow corn meal
5ml/1 tsp salt
5ml/1 tsp chilli powder
4 large (US extra large) eggs
900ml/1½ pint/3¾ cups milk
50g/2oz/4 tbsp butter, melted
vegetable oil, for greasing

For the filling
60ml/4 tbsp olive oil
900g/2lb butternut squash (peeled
weight), seeded and diced
large pinch of dried red chilli flakes
4 large leeks, thickly sliced
5ml/1 tsp chopped fresh thyme
6 chicory heads, thickly sliced
225g/8oz goat's cheese, cut into cubes
200g/7oz walnuts, roughly chopped
60ml/4 tbsp chopped flat leaf parsley
50g/2oz Parmesan cheese, grated
90ml/6 tbsp melted butter or olive oil
salt and ground black pepper

1 Sift the flour, corn meal, salt and chilli powder into a bowl and make a well in the centre. Add the eggs and a little milk. Whisk the eggs and milk, mixing the dry ingredients and adding more milk as the mixture comes together.

2 When ready to cook the pancakes, whisk the melted butter into the batter. Heat a lightly greased or oiled 18cm/7in heavy frying pan or crêpe pan. Pour about 60ml/4 tbsp batter into the pan and cook for 2–3 minutes, until set and lightly browned underneath. Turn and cook the pancake on the second side for 2–3 minutes. Lightly grease the pan after every second pancake.

3 To make the filling, heat the oil in a large frying pan. Add the squash and cook, stirring frequently, for 10 minutes, until almost tender. Add the chilli flakes and cook, stirring, for 1–2 minutes. Stir in the leeks and thyme and cook for another 4–5 minutes.

4 Add the chicory and cook, stirring often, for another 4–5 minutes, until the leeks are cooked and the chicory is hot, but still has some bite to its texture. Cool slightly, then stir in the cheese, walnuts and parsley. Season the mixture.

5 Preheat the oven to 200°C/400°F/ Gas 6. Lightly grease an ovenproof dish. Spoon 30–45ml/2–3 tbsp filling on to each pancake. Roll or fold each pancake to enclose the filling, then place in the prepared dish.

6 Sprinkle the Parmesan over the pancakes and drizzle the melted butter or olive oil over. Bake for 10–15 minutes, until the cheese is bubbling. Serve hot.

Coquilles St Jacques

A classic French first course that calls for the best quality scallops possible to ensure a truly wonderful result. Select firm, white shellfish and check that they have not previously been frozen before buying them to ensure they are not watery and flabby. You will need eight scallop shells to serve this dish.

Serves 8

900g/2lb potatoes, chopped
115g/4oz/¹⁄₂ cup butter
8 large or 16 small scallops
250ml/8fl oz/1 cup fish stock

For the sauce
50g/2oz/4 tbsp butter
50g/2oz/¹⁄₂ cup plain (all-purpose) flour
600ml/1 pint/2¹⁄₂ cups milk
60ml/4 tbsp single (light) cream
250g/8oz/2 cups grated mature (sharp)
 Cheddar cheese
salt and ground black pepper
dill sprigs, to garnish
grilled (broiled) lemon wedges, to serve

1 Preheat oven to 200°C/400°F/Gas 6. Place the chopped potatoes in a large pan, cover with lightly salted water and boil for 15 minutes, or until tender. Drain and mash with the butter.

2 Spoon the mixture into a piping (pastry) bag fitted with a star nozzle. Pipe the potatoes around the outside of a cleaned scallop shell. Repeat the process, making eight in total.

3 Simmer the scallops in the fish stock for about 3 minutes, or until just firm. Do not allow the stock to boil but poach the scallops gently otherwise they will become tough and rubbery. Drain and slice the scallops finely. Set them aside.

4 To make the sauce, melt the butter in a small pan, add the flour and cook over a low heat for a couple of minutes, gradually add the milk and cream, stirring constantly and cook until thickened.

5 Stir in the cheese and cook until melted. Season to taste. Spoon a little sauce in the base of each shell. Divide the scallops between the shells and then pour the remaining sauce over the scallops.

6 Bake the scallops for 10 minutes, or until golden. Garnish with dill and serve with grilled lemon wedges.

Crab Salad with Rocket

Garnish these salads with strips of lemon rind, if you like.

Serves 8

8 dressed crabs
2 red (bell) peppers, seeded
   and chopped
2 small red onions, finely chopped
60ml/4 tbsp fresh coriander (cilantro)
60ml/4 tbsp drained capers
grated rind and juice of 3 lemons
Tabasco sauce, to taste
salt and ground black pepper

For the salad
75g/3oz rocket (arugula) leaves
60ml/4 tbsp sunflower oil
30ml/2 tbsp fresh lime juice

1 Remove all the white and brown meat from the crab. Put it into a large mixing bowl with the chopped peppers, onions and coriander. Add the capers, lemon rind and juice, and toss gently to mix everything thoroughly together. Season with a few drops of Tabasco sauce, according to taste, and a little salt and pepper.

2 To make the salad, wash the rocket leaves and pat them dry on kitchen paper. Divide between eight plates. Mix together the oil and lime juice in a small bowl. Dress the rocket leaves with the oil and lime juice.

3 Pile the crab salad on top and serve garnished with lemon rind strips.

Pork and Bacon Rillettes with Onion Salad

Rillettes is potted meat from pork and ham. This version makes a great appetizer or light meal.

Serves 8

1.8kg/4lb belly of pork, boned and cut into cubes (reserve the bones)
450g/1lb rindless streaky (fatty) bacon, finely chopped
5ml/1 tsp salt
1.5ml/¼ tsp freshly ground black pepper
4 garlic cloves, finely chopped
2 fresh parsley sprigs
1 bay leaf
2 fresh thyme sprigs
1 fresh sage sprig
300ml/½ pint/1¼ cups water
crusty French bread, to serve

For the onion salad
1 small red onion, halved and finely sliced
2 spring onions (scallions), cut into matchstick strips
2 celery sticks, cut into matchstick strips
15ml/1 tbsp freshly squeezed lemon juice
15ml/1 tbsp light olive oil
ground black pepper

1 In a bowl, mix the pork, bacon and salt. Cover and leave for 30 minutes. Preheat the oven to 150°C/300°F/Gas 2. Stir the pepper and garlic into the meat. Tie the herbs together to make a bouquet garni and add to the meat.

2 Spread the meat mixture in a roasting pan and pour in the water. Place the bones from the pork on top and cover tightly with foil. Cook for 3½ hours.

3 Discard the bones and herbs, and ladle the meat mixture into a metal sieve set over a large bowl. Allow the liquid to drain through into the bowl, then turn the meat into a shallow dish. Repeat until all the meat is drained. Reserve the liquid. Use two forks to pull the meat apart into fine shreds.

4 Line a 1.5 litre/2½ pint/6¼ cup terrine or deep, straight-sided dish with clear film (plastic wrap) and spoon in the shredded meat. Strain the reserved liquid through a sieve lined with muslin (cheesecloth) and pour it over the meat. Leave to cool. Cover and chill in the fridge for at least 24 hours, or until set.

5 To make the onion salad, place the sliced onion, spring onions and celery in a bowl. Add the freshly squeezed lemon juice and light olive oil and toss gently. Season with a little freshly ground black pepper, but do not add any salt as the rillettes is well salted.

6 Serve the rillettes, cut into thick slices, on individual plates with a little onion salad and thick slices of crusty French bread.

Chicken Liver Pâté with Garlic

This smooth pâté is wickedly indulgent but absolutely delicious. Start preparation the day before so that the flavour can develop fully.

Serves 6 to 8

225g/8oz/1 cup unsalted (sweet) butter
400g/14oz chicken livers, chopped
45–60ml/3–4 tbsp Madeira
3 large shallots, chopped
2 large garlic cloves, finely chopped
5ml/1 tsp finely chopped fresh thyme
pinch of ground allspice
30ml/2 tbsp double (heavy)
*   cream (optional)*
salt and ground black pepper
small fresh bay leaves or fresh thyme
*   sprigs, to garnish*
toast and small pickled gherkins,
*   to serve*

1 Melt 75g/3oz/6 tbsp butter in a small pan over a low heat, then allow it to bubble gently until it is clear. Pour off the clarified butter into a bowl.

2 Melt 40g/1½ oz/3 tbsp butter in a frying pan and fry the chicken livers for 4–5 minutes, or until browned. Stir frequently to ensure that the livers cook evenly. Do not overcook them or they will be tough.

3 Add 45ml/3 tbsp Madeira and set it alight, then scrape the contents of the pan into a food processor or blender.

4 Melt 25g/1oz/2 tbsp butter in the pan over a low heat and cook the shallots for 5 minutes, or until soft. Add the garlic, thyme and allspice and cook for another 2–3 minutes. Add this mixture to the livers with the remaining butter and cream, if using, then process until smooth.

5 Add about 7.5ml/1½ tsp each of salt and black pepper and more Madeira to taste. Scrape the pâté into a serving dish and place a few bay leaves or thyme sprigs on top. Melt the clarified butter, if necessary, then pour it over the pâté. Cool and chill the pâté for 4 hours or overnight.

VARIATIONS
• Cognac, Armagnac or port can be used instead of the Madeira.
• Use duck livers instead of chicken and add 2.5ml/½ tsp grated orange rind.
• Use chopped fresh tarragon instead of the thyme.

Prosciutto with Potato Rémoulade

Lime juice brings a contemporary twist to this cream-enriched version of the classic piquant rémoulade dressing. It is best made when the new season's asparagus is available.

Serves 8

4 potatoes, each weighing about
   350g/12oz, quartered lengthways
300ml/½ pint/1¼ cup mayonnaise
300ml/½ pint/1¼ cup double
   (heavy) cream
10–15ml/2–3 tsp Dijon mustard
juice of 1 lime
60ml/4 tbsp olive oil
24 prosciutto slices
900g/2lb asparagus spears, halved
salt and ground black pepper
50g/2oz wild rocket (arugula),
   to garnish
extra virgin olive oil, to serve

1 Put the potatoes in a pan. Add water to cover and bring to the boil. Add salt, then simmer for about 15 minutes, or until the potatoes are tender, but do not let them get too soft. Drain thoroughly and leave to cool and then cut into long, thin strips.

2 Beat together the mayonnaise, cream, mustard, lime juice and seasoning in a large bowl. Add the potatoes and stir carefully to coat them with the dressing.

3 Heat the oil in a griddle or frying pan and cook the prosciutto in batches until crisp and golden. Use a slotted spoon to remove, draining each piece well.

4 Cook the asparagus in the fat remaining in the pan for 3 minutes, or until tender and golden.

5 Put a generous spoonful of potato rémoulade on each plate and top with several slices of prosciutto. Add the asparagus and garnish with rocket. Serve immediately, offering olive oil to drizzle over.

VARIATION
Use a mixture of potatoes and celeriac instead of all potatoes. For an inexpensive salad use mixed root vegetables and omit the asparagus, adding fresh or roasted cherry tomatoes instead.

dinner party and festive main courses

Classic dishes are sure winners for dinner parties

and celebrations, especially with a clever twist

of seasoning or a contemporary garnish.

Roasted Garlic and Aubergine Custards with Red Pepper Dressing

These make a splendid main course for a special vegetarian dinner. Serve fresh, warm bread and steamed broccoli as accompaniments.

Serves 6

2 large heads of garlic
6–7 fresh thyme sprigs
60ml/4 tbsp extra virgin olive oil, plus
*   extra for greasing*
350g/12oz aubergines (eggplant),
*   cut into 1cm/½in dice*
2 large red (bell) peppers, halved
*   and seeded*
pinch of saffron threads
300ml/½ pint/1¼ cups whipping cream
2 large (US extra large) eggs
pinch of caster (superfine) sugar
30ml/2 tbsp shredded fresh basil leaves
salt and ground black pepper

For the dressing
90ml/6 tbsp extra virgin oil
15–25ml/1–1½ tbsp balsamic vinegar
pinch of caster (superfine) sugar
115g/4oz tomatoes, peeled, seeded
*   and finely diced*
½ small red onion, finely chopped
generous pinch of ground toasted
*   cumin seeds*
handful of fresh basil leaves

1 Preheat the oven to 190°C/375°F/Gas 5. Place the garlic on a piece of foil with the thyme and sprinkle with 15ml/1 tbsp of the oil. Wrap the foil around the garlic and cook for 35–45 minutes, or until the garlic is soft. Cool slightly. Reduce the oven temperature to 180°C/350°F/Gas 4.

2 Meanwhile, heat the remaining olive oil in a heavy pan. Add the diced aubergines and fry over a medium heat, stirring frequently, for 5–8 minutes, or until they are browned and cooked.

3 Grill (broil) the peppers, skin sides uppermost, until they are black. Place the peppers in a bowl, cover and leave for 10 minutes.

4 When the peppers are cool enough to handle, peel and dice them. Soak the saffron in 15ml/1 tbsp hot water for 10 minutes.

5 Unwrap the roasted garlic and separate the cloves, then squeeze the flesh out of its skin into a blender or food processor. Discard the thyme sprigs. Add the oil from cooking the garlic, the cream and eggs to the garlic. Process until smooth. Add the soaked saffron with its liquid, and season well with salt, pepper and a pinch of sugar. Stir in half the diced red pepper and the shredded basil leaves.

6 Lightly grease six large ovenproof ramekins (about 200–250ml/7–8fl oz/1 cup capacity) and line the base of each with a circle of baking parchment. Grease the baking parchment.

7 Divide the aubergines among the dishes. Pour the egg mixture into the ramekins, then place them in a roasting pan. Cover each dish with foil and make a little hole in the centre of the foil to allow steam to escape. Pour hot water into the tin to come halfway up the outsides of the ramekins. Bake for 25–30 minutes, or until the custards are just set in the centre.

8 Make the dressing while the custards are cooking. Whisk the oil and vinegar with salt, pepper and a pinch of sugar. Stir in the tomatoes, red onion, remaining red pepper and cumin. Set aside some of the basil leaves for garnishing, then chop the rest and add to the dressing.

9 Leave the custards to cool for about 5 minutes. Slide a knife around the insides of the ramekins and invert the custards on to warmed serving plates. Spoon the dressing around the custards and garnish each with the reserved fresh basil leaves.

Goat's Cheese Soufflé

The mellow flavour of roasted garlic pervades this simple, but elegant soufflé. Balance the rich soufflé with a crisp green salad, including peppery leaves.

Serves 6 to 8

4 large heads of garlic
6 fresh thyme sprigs
30ml/2 tbsp olive oil
475ml/16fl oz/2 cups milk
2 fresh bay leaves
4 x 1cm/½in thick onion slices
4 cloves
115g/4oz/½ cup butter
75g/3oz/⅔ cup plain (all-purpose)
 flour, sifted
cayenne pepper
6 eggs, separated, plus 1 egg white
300g/11oz goat's cheese, crumbled
115g/4oz/1¼ cups freshly grated
 Parmesan cheese
5–10ml/1–2 tsp chopped fresh thyme
5ml/1 tsp cream of tartar
salt and ground black pepper

1 Preheat the oven to 180°C/350°F/ Gas 4. Place the garlic and thyme sprigs on a piece of foil. Sprinkle with the oil and close the foil around the garlic, then bake for about 1 hour, until the garlic is soft. Leave to cool.

2 Squeeze the garlic out of its skin. Discard the thyme and garlic skins, then purée the garlic flesh with the oil.

3 Meanwhile, place the milk, bay leaves, onion slices and cloves in a medium pan. Bring to the boil, then remove from the heat. Cover and leave to stand for 30 minutes.

4 Melt 75g/3oz/6 tbsp of the butter in another pan. Stir in the flour and cook gently for 2 minutes, stirring. Reheat and strain the milk, then slowly stir it into the flour and butter.

5 Cook the sauce very gently for 10 minutes, stirring frequently. Season with salt, pepper and a pinch of cayenne. Cool slightly. Preheat the oven to 200°C/400°F/Gas 6.

6 Beat the egg yolks into the sauce one at a time. Then beat in the goat's cheese, all but 30ml/2 tbsp of the Parmesan and the chopped thyme. Use the remaining butter to grease a large soufflé dish (1 litre/1¾ pints/4 cups) or eight ramekins (about 125ml/4fl oz/½ cup).

7 Whisk the egg whites and cream of tartar in a scrupulously clean bowl until firm, but not dry. Stir 90ml/6 tbsp of the egg whites into the sauce, then gently, but thoroughly, fold in the remainder using a rubber spatula.

8 Pour the mixture into the prepared dish or dishes. Run a knife around the edge of each dish, pushing the mixture away from the rim. Sprinkle with the reserved Parmesan.

9 Place the dish or dishes on a baking sheet and cook for 25–30 minutes for a large soufflé or 20 minutes for small soufflés. The mixture should be risen and firm to a light touch in the centre; it should not wobble excessively when given a light push. Serve immediately.

COOK'S TIP

Whisked egg whites give a soufflé its characteristic airy texture. But the lightness can be destroyed if they are folded in too roughly. Fold whites in using a rubber spatula and a cutting and scooping action. Turn the bowl a little after each stroke.

Peppers filled with **Spiced Vegetables**

Indian spices season the potato and aubergine stuffing in these colourful baked peppers. They are good with plain rice and a lentil dhal, or a salad, Indian breads and a cucumber or mint and yogurt raita.

Serves 6

*6 large evenly shaped red or yellow
   (bell) peppers*
500g/1¼lb waxy potatoes
1 small onion, chopped
4–5 garlic cloves, chopped
*5cm/2in piece fresh root
   ginger, chopped*
*1–2 fresh green chillies, seeded
   and chopped*
105ml/7 tbsp water
*90–105ml/6–7 tbsp groundnut
   (peanut) oil*
*1 aubergine (eggplant), cut into
   1cm/½in dice*
10ml/2 tsp cumin seeds
5ml/1 tsp kalonji (nigella) seeds
2.5ml/½ tsp ground turmeric
5ml/1 tsp ground coriander
5ml/1 tsp ground toasted cumin seeds
pinch of cayenne pepper
about 30ml/2 tbsp lemon juice
salt and ground black pepper
*30ml/2 tbsp chopped fresh coriander
   (cilantro), to garnish*

1 Cut the tops off the red or yellow peppers then remove and discard the seeds. Cut a thin slice off the base of the peppers, if necessary, to make them stand upright.

2 Bring a large saucepan of lightly salted water to the boil. Add the peppers and cook for 5–6 minutes. Drain and leave the peppers upside down in a colander.

3 Cook the potatoes in boiling, salted water for 10–12 minutes, until just tender. Drain, cool and peel, then cut into 1cm/½in dice.

4 Put the onion, garlic, ginger and green chillies in a food processor or blender with 60ml/4 tbsp of the water and process to a purée.

5 Heat 45ml/3 tbsp of the oil in a large, deep frying pan and cook the aubergine, stirring occasionally, until browned on all sides. Remove from the pan and set aside. Add another 30ml/ 2 tbsp of the oil to the pan and cook the potatoes until lightly browned. Remove from the pan and set aside.

6 If necessary, add another 15ml/1 tbsp oil to the pan, then add the cumin and kalonji seeds. Fry briefly until the seeds darken, then add the turmeric, coriander and ground cumin. Cook for 15 seconds. Stir in the onion and garlic purée and fry, scraping the pan with a spatula, until it begins to brown.

7 Return the potatoes and aubergines to the pan, season with salt, pepper and 1–2 pinches of cayenne. Add the remaining water and 15ml/1 tbsp lemon juice and then cook, stirring, until the liquid evaporates. Preheat the oven to 190°C/375°F/Gas 5.

8 Fill the peppers with the potato mix and place on a lightly greased baking tray. Brush the peppers with a little oil and bake for 30–35 minutes, until the peppers are cooked. Allow to cool, then sprinkle with a little more lemon juice, garnish with the coriander and serve.

Fillets of Sea Bream in Filo Pastry

Any firm fish fillets can be used for this dish. Each little parcel is a meal in itself and can be prepared several hours in advance, which makes them ideal for entertaining.

Serves 8

16 small waxy salad potatoes
400g/14oz sorrel, stalks removed
60ml/4 tbsp olive oil
32 sheets of filo pastry, thawed
    if frozen
8 sea bream fillets, about 175g/6oz
    each, scaled but not skinned
115g/4oz/½ cup butter, melted
250ml/8fl oz/1 cup fish stock
475ml/16fl oz/2 cups double
    (heavy) cream
salt and ground black pepper
finely diced red (bell) pepper, to garnish

1 Preheat the oven to 200°C/400°F/ Gas 6. Cook the salad potatoes in lightly salted boiling water for 15–20 minutes, or until just tender. Drain and set aside to cool.

2 Shred half the sorrel leaves by piling up six or eight at a time, rolling them up like a fat cigar and cutting them with a sharp knife, into very fine slices: shake these out.

3 Thinly slice the potatoes lengthways. Brush a baking tray with a little oil. Lay a sheet of filo pastry on the tray, brush it with oil then lay a second sheet crossways over the first. Repeat with two more sheets. Arrange one-eighth of the sliced potatoes in the centre of the pastry, season well and add one-eighth of the shredded sorrel. Lay a bream fillet on top, skin side up. Season to taste again.

4 Loosely fold the filo pastry up and over to make a neat parcel. Make seven more parcels in the same way. Place on the baking tray and brush them with half the butter. Bake for 20 minutes, or until the filo has fully puffed up and is golden brown.

5 Meanwhile, make the sorrel sauce. Heat the remaining butter in a small pan, add the reserved sorrel and cook until it wilts. Stir in the fish stock and cream. Heat almost to boiling point, stirring constantly. Season and keep hot. Serve the fish parcels garnished with red pepper and offer the sauce separately in its own bowl.

Lobster Thermidor

One of the classic French dishes, lobster thermidor makes a little lobster go a long way. It is best to use large lobsters rather than small ones, as they will contain a higher proportion of flesh and the meat will be sweeter.

Serves 6

3 large lobsters, about
  800g–1kg/1¾–2¼lb, boiled
120ml/4fl oz/½ cup brandy
75g/3oz/6 tbsp butter
6 shallots, finely chopped
350g/12oz/4½ cups button (white)
  mushrooms, thinly sliced
50ml/3 tbsp plain (all-purpose) flour
350ml/12fl oz/1½ cups fish stock
350ml/12fl oz/1½ cups double
  (heavy) cream
15ml/1 tbsp Dijon mustard
6 egg yolks, beaten
120ml/9 tbsp dry white wine
115g/4oz/1¼ cups freshly grated
  Parmesan cheese
salt, ground black pepper and
  cayenne pepper
steamed rice and salad leaves, to serve

1 Split each lobster in half lengthways; crack the claws. Discard the stomach sac, and keep the coral for another dish. Keeping each half-shell intact, extract the meat from the tail and claws, then cut into large dice. Place in a shallow dish; sprinkle over the brandy. Cover and set aside. Wipe and dry the half-shells and set them aside.

2 Melt the butter in a pan and cook the shallots over a low heat until soft. Add the mushrooms and cook until just tender, stirring constantly. Stir in the flour and a pinch of cayenne pepper; cook, stirring, for 2–3 minutes. Gradually add the stock, stirring until the sauce boils and thickens.

3 Stir in the cream and mustard and continue to cook until the sauce is smooth and thick. Season to taste with salt, black pepper and cayenne. Pour half the sauce on to the egg yolks, stir well and return the mixture to the pan. Stir in the wine. Taste and adjust the seasoning, being generous with the cayenne pepper.

4 Preheat the grill (broiler) to medium-high. Stir the diced lobster and the brandy into the sauce. Arrange the lobster half-shells in a grill pan and divide the mixture among them. Sprinkle with Parmesan and place under the grill until browned. Serve with the rice and salad leaves.

Boeuf Bourguignonne

This classic French dish of beef cooked in Burgundy style with red wine, small pieces of bacon, baby onions and mushrooms, is a favourite choice for a dinner party.

Serves 6

175g/6oz rindless streaky (fatty) bacon
  rashers (strips), chopped
900g/2lb lean braising steak, such as
  top rump of beef or braising steak
30ml/2 tbsp plain (all-purpose) flour
45ml/3 tbsp sunflower oil
25g/1oz/2 tbsp butter
12 shallots
2 garlic cloves, crushed
175g/6oz/2⅓ cups mushrooms, sliced
450ml/¾ pint/scant 2 cups red wine
150ml/¼ pint/⅔ cup beef stock
  or consommé
1 bay leaf
2 sprigs each of fresh thyme, parsley
  and marjoram
salt and ground black pepper
creamed potatoes and celeriac, to serve

1 Preheat the oven to 160°C/325°F/ Gas 3. Heat a large flameproof casserole, then add the bacon and cook, stirring occasionally, until the fat runs and the cooked pieces are crisp and golden brown.

2 Meanwhile, cut the meat into 2.5cm/1in cubes. Season the flour and use to coat the meat. Use a slotted spoon to remove the bacon from the casserole and set aside. Add and heat the oil, then brown the beef in batches and set aside with the bacon (cooking too much at once reduces the temperature of the oil drastically).

3 Add the butter to the fat remaining in the casserole. Cook the shallots and garlic until just starting to colour, then add the mushrooms and cook for a further 5 minutes. Replace the bacon and meat, and stir in the wine and stock or consommé. Tie the bay leaf, thyme, parsley and marjoram together into a bouquet garni and add to the casserole.

4 Cover and cook in the oven for 1½ hours, or until the meat is tender, stirring once or twice. Season to taste and serve the casserole with creamy mashed root vegetables, such as celeriac and potatoes.

Beef Wellington

Tender fillet of beef baked in puff pastry makes a sophisticated main course for a formal dinner. Start preparing the dish well in advance to allow time for the meat to cool before it is wrapped in the pastry.

Serves 6

1.5kg/3¼lb fillet of beef
45ml/3 tbsp sunflower oil
115g/4oz/1½ cups mushrooms, chopped
2 garlic cloves, crushed
175g/6oz smooth liver pâté
30ml/2 tbsp chopped fresh parsley
400g/14oz puff pastry
beaten egg, to glaze
salt and ground black pepper
fresh flat leaf parsley, to garnish

1 Tie the fillet of beef at regular intervals with string so that it stays in a neat shape during cooking.

2 Heat 30ml/2 tbsp of the sunflower oil in a large frying pan, and fry the beef over a high heat for about 10 minutes, until brown on all sides. Transfer to a roasting pan, bake for 20 minutes. Allow to cool.

3 Heat the remaining oil in a frying pan and cook the mushrooms and garlic for about 5 minutes. Beat the mushroom mixture into the pâté with the parsley, season well. Set aside to cool.

4 Roll out the pastry into a sheet large enough to enclose the beef, plus a strip to spare. Trim off the spare pastry, trim the other edges to neaten. Spread the pâté mix down the middle of the pastry. Untie the beef and lay it on the pâté.

5 Preheat the oven to 220°C/425°F/Gas 7. Brush the edges of the pastry with beaten egg and fold the pastry over the meat to enclose it in a neat parcel. Place the parcel on a baking tray with the join in the pastry underneath. Cut leaf shapes from the reserved pastry. Brush the parcel with egg, garnish with pastry leaves. Chill for 10 minutes.

6 Bake the Beef Wellington for 50–60 minutes, covering it loosely with foil after about 30 minutes to prevent the pastry from burning. Serve cut into thick slices garnished with parsley.

Tagine of Lamb with Couscous

A tagine is a classic Moroccan stew which is traditionally served with couscous. Its warm and fruity flavourings create a rich and flavoursome sauce that is perfect for serving at winter-evening dinner parties.

Serves 6

*1kg/2¼lb lean boneless lamb,
  such as shoulder or neck fillet*
25g/1oz/2 tbsp butter
15ml/1 tbsp sunflower oil
1 large onion, chopped
2 garlic cloves, chopped
*2.5cm/1in piece fresh root ginger,
  peeled and finely chopped*
*1 red (bell) pepper, seeded
  and chopped*
*900ml/1½ pints/3¾ cups lamb stock
  or water*
*250g/9oz/generous 1 cup
  ready-to-eat prunes*
juice of 1 lemon
15ml/1 tbsp clear honey
1.5ml/¼ tsp saffron threads
1 cinnamon stick, broken in half
*50g/2oz/½ cup flaked (sliced)
  almonds, toasted*
salt and ground black pepper

To serve
450g/1lb/2⅔ cups couscous
25g/1oz/2 tbsp butter
*30ml/2 tbsp chopped fresh
  coriander (cilantro)*

1 Trim the lamb and cut it into 2.5cm/1in cubes. Heat the butter and oil in a large flameproof casserole until foaming. Add the onion, garlic and ginger and cook, stirring occasionally, until softened but not coloured.

2 Add the lamb and red pepper and mix well. (The meat is not sealed in batches over high heat for an authentic tagine.) Pour in the stock or water.

3 Add the prunes, lemon juice, honey, saffron threads and cinnamon. Season to taste with salt and pepper and stir well. Bring to the boil, then reduce the heat and cover the casserole. Simmer for 1½–2 hours, stirring occasionally, or until the meat is melt-in-the-mouth tender.

4 Meanwhile, cook the couscous according to packet instructions, usually by placing in a large bowl and pouring in boiling water to cover the "grains" by 2.5cm/1in. Stir well, then cover and leave to stand for 5–10 minutes. The couscous absorbs the water and swells to become tender and fluffy. Stir in the butter, chopped fresh coriander and seasoning to taste.

5 Taste the stew for seasoning and add more salt and pepper if necessary. Pile the couscous into a large, warmed serving dish or on to individual warmed bowls or plates. Ladle the stew on to the couscous and sprinkle the toasted flaked almonds over the top.

Medallions of Venison with Herby Horseradish Dumplings

Venison is lean and full-flavoured, and tastes great with these piquant dumplings. This recipe makes an attractive dinner party dish.

Serves 8

1.2 litres/2 pints/5 cups venison stock
250ml/8fl oz/1 cup port
30ml/2 tbsp sunflower oil
8 medallions of venison, about
    175g/6oz each
chopped fresh parsley, to garnish
steamed baby vegetables, to serve

For the dumplings
150g/5oz/1¼ cup self-raising
    (self-rising) flour
75g/3oz beef suet (US grated shortening)
30ml/2 tbsp chopped mixed herbs
10ml/2 tsp creamed horseradish
90–120ml/6–8 tbsp water

1 First make the dumplings: mix the flour, suet and herbs and make a well in the middle. Add the horseradish and water, then mix to make a soft but not sticky dough. Shape the dough into walnut-sized balls and chill in the refrigerator for up to 1 hour.

2 Boil the venison stock in a pan until reduced by half. Add the port and continue boiling until reduced again by half, then pour the reduced stock into a frying pan. Heat the stock until it is simmering and add the dumplings. Poach them for 5–10 minutes, or until risen and cooked through. Use a slotted spoon to remove the dumplings.

COOK'S TIP
Serve a variety of steamed vegetables with the venison such as carrots, courgettes (zucchini) and turnips.

3 Smear the sunflower oil over a non-stick griddle, heat until very hot. Add the venison, cook for 2–3 minutes on each side. Place the venison medallions on warmed serving plates and pour the sauce over. Serve with the dumplings and vegetables, garnished with parsley.

VARIATION
Beef fillet medallions can be used instead of the venison. Replace the venison stock with beef stock.

Herb-crusted Rack of Lamb with Puy Lentils

This roast is quick and easy to prepare, yet impressive when served: the perfect choice when entertaining.

Serves 8

4 × 6-bone racks of lamb, chined
115g/4oz/2 cups fresh white
    breadcrumbs
4 large garlic cloves, crushed
40g/1½ oz chopped mixed fresh herbs,
    such as rosemary, thyme, flat leaf
    parsley and marjoram, plus extra
    sprigs to garnish
115g/4oz/½ cup butter, melted
salt and ground black pepper

For the Puy lentils
2 red onions, chopped
60ml/4 tbsp olive oil
2 × 400g/14oz cans Puy or green
    lentils, rinsed and drained
2 × 400g/14oz cans chopped tomatoes
60ml/4 tbsp chopped fresh parsley

1 Preheat the oven to 220°C/425°F/ Gas 7. Trim off any excess fat from the racks of lamb, and season well with salt and ground black pepper.

2 Mix together the breadcrumbs, garlic, herbs and butter, and press on to the fat-sides of the lamb. Place in a roasting pan and roast for 25 minutes. Cover with foil; stand for 5 minutes before carving.

COOK'S TIP
Boiled or steamed new potatoes and broccoli are good accompaniments.

3 To make the Puy lentils, cook the onion in the olive oil until softened. Add the lentils and tomatoes and cook gently for 5 minutes, or until the lentils are piping hot. Stir in the parsley and season to taste.

4 Cut each rack of lamb in half and serve with the lentils. Garnish with the extra herb sprigs.

VARIATION
Add the grated rind of 1 lemon and 30ml/2 tbsp finely chopped walnuts to the crumb mixture.

Glazed Poussins

Golden poussins make an impressive main course. Serve them with traditional roast accompaniments or a refreshing side salad.

Serves 6

75g/3oz/6 tbsp butter
15ml/1 tbsp mixed (pumpkin pie) spice
45ml/3 tbsp clear honey
grated rind and juice of 3 clementines
6 poussins, each weighing about
    450g/1lb
1 large onion, finely chopped
2 garlic cloves, chopped
25ml/1½ tbsp plain (all-purpose) flour
75ml/2½ fl oz/⅓ cup Marsala
450ml/¾ pint/scant 2 cups
    chicken stock
bunch of fresh coriander (cilantro),
    to garnish

VARIATION

You can stuff each poussin, before roasting, with a quartered clementine.

1 Preheat the oven to 220°C/425°F/ Gas 7. To make the glaze, heat the butter, mixed spice, honey and clementine rind and juice until the butter has melted, stirring to mix well. Remove from the heat.

2 Place the poussins in a large roasting pan, brush them with the glaze, then roast for 40 minutes. Brush with any remaining glaze and baste occasionally with the pan juices during cooking. Transfer the poussins to a serving platter, cover with foil and leave to stand for 10 minutes.

3 Skim off all but 15ml/1 tbsp of the fat from the roasting pan. Add the onion and garlic to the juices in the pan and cook on the stove, stirring occasionally, until beginning to brown. Stir in the flour, then gradually pour in the Marsala, followed by the stock, whisking constantly. Bring to the boil and simmer for 3 minutes to make a smooth, rich gravy.

4 Transfer the poussins to warm plates or leave on the serving platter and garnish with coriander. Serve at once, offering the gravy separately.

Roast Goose with Caramelized Apples

Tender goose served with sweet apples makes this a perfect celebration main course.

Serves 8

4.5–5.5kg/10–12lb goose, with giblets, thawed, if frozen
salt and ground black pepper

For the apple and nut stuffing

225g/8oz/1 cup prunes
150ml/¼ pint/⅔ cup port or red wine
675g/1½lb cooking apples, peeled and cored
1 large onion, chopped
4 celery sticks, sliced
15ml/1 tbsp mixed dried herbs
finely grated rind of 1 orange
goose liver, chopped
450g/1lb pork sausage meat (bulk sausage)
115g/4oz/1 cup chopped pecan nuts
2 eggs

For the caramelized apples

50g/2oz/¼ cup butter
60ml/4 tbsp redcurrant jelly
30ml/2 tbsp red wine vinegar
9 small eating apples, peeled and cored

For the gravy

30ml/2 tbsp plain (all-purpose) flour
600ml/1 pint/2½ cups giblet stock
juice of 1 orange

1 Soak the prunes in the port or red wine for 24 hours. Stone (pit) and cut each prune into four. Reserve the liquid.

2 The next day, mix the prunes with all the remaining stuffing ingredients and season well. Moisten with half the reserved port or red wine.

3 Preheat the oven to 200°C/400°F/Gas 6. Stuff the neck-end of the goose, tucking the flap of skin under and securing it with a small skewer. Remove the excess fat from the cavity and pack it with the stuffing. Tie the legs together to hold them in place.

4 Weigh the stuffed goose to calculate the cooking time: allow 15 minutes for each 450g/1lb plus 15 minutes over. Put the bird on a rack in a roasting pan and rub the skin with salt. Prick the skin all over to help the fat run out. Roast for 30 minutes, then reduce the heat to 180°C/350°F/Gas 4 and roast for the remaining cooking time. Occasionally check and pour off any fat produced during cooking into a bowl. The goose is cooked when the juices run clear when the thickest part of the thigh is pierced with a skewer. Pour a little cold water over the breast halfway through the cooking time to crisp up the skin.

5 Meanwhile, prepare the apples. Melt the butter, redcurrant jelly and vinegar in a small roasting pan or a shallow ovenproof dish. Put in the apples, baste them well and cook in the oven for 15–20 minutes. Baste the apples halfway through the cooking time. Do not cover them or they will collapse.

6 Lift the goose on to the serving dish and let it stand for 15 minutes before carving. Pour off the excess fat from the roasting pan, leaving any sediment in the bottom. Stir in the flour, cook gently until brown, and then blend in the stock. Bring to the boil, add the remaining reserved port, orange juice and seasoning. Simmer for 2–3 minutes. Strain into a gravy boat.

7 Surround the goose with the caramelized apples and spoon over the redcurrant glaze. Serve with the gravy.

COOK'S TIP

Do not overestimate the yield from a goose – the bird often looks big but there is a lot of fat and not too much meat on it for its size.

Roasted Stuffed Turkey

Serve this classic roast with stuffing balls, bacon rolls, roast potatoes, vegetables and gravy.

Serves 8

4.5kg/10lb oven-ready turkey, with
* giblets, thawed, if frozen*
1 large onion, peeled and studded
* with 6 whole cloves*
50g/2oz/¼ cup butter, softened
10 chipolata sausages
salt and ground black pepper

For the stuffing
225g/8oz rindless streaky (fatty)
* bacon, chopped*
1 large onion, finely chopped
450g/1lb pork sausage meat
* (bulk sausage)*
25g/1oz/⅓ cup rolled oats
30ml/2 tbsp chopped fresh parsley
10ml/2 tsp dried mixed herbs
1 large (US extra large) egg, beaten
115g/4oz/1 cup ready-to-eat dried
* apricots, finely chopped*

For the gravy
25g/1oz/¼ cup plain (all-purpose) flour
450ml/¾ pint/scant 2 cups giblet stock

1 Preheat the oven to 200°C/400°F/ Gas 6. To make the stuffing, cook the bacon and onion over a gentle heat in a frying pan until the bacon is crisp and the onion is tender but not browned. Transfer to a large bowl and add the remaining stuffing ingredients. Season well and mix to combine.

2 Stuff the neck end of the turkey only, tucking the flap of skin under and securing it with a small skewer or stitching it in place with a thread. Do not overstuff the turkey or the skin will burst during cooking. Reserve any remaining stuffing and set aside.

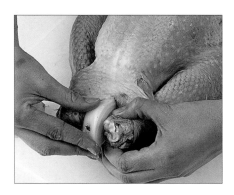

3 Put the onion studded with cloves in the body cavity of the turkey and tie the legs together with string to hold them in place. Weigh the stuffed bird and calculate the cooking time: allow 15 minutes per 450g/1lb plus 15 minutes over. Place the turkey in a large roasting pan.

4 Brush the turkey with the butter and season well with salt and pepper. Cover it loosely with foil and cook it for 30 minutes. Baste the turkey with the pan juices. Then lower the oven temperature to 180°C/350°F/Gas 4 and cook for the remainder of the calculated cooking time. Baste the turkey every 30 minutes or so and check for any small bubbles of fat, pricking them with a fork to release the fat from the skin.

5 Remove the foil from the turkey for the last hour of cooking and baste. With wet hands, shape the remaining stuffing into small balls or pack it into a greased ovenproof dish. Cook in the oven for 20 minutes, or until golden brown and crisp. About 20 minutes before the end of cooking, put the chipolata sausages into an ovenproof dish and put them in the oven. The turkey is cooked if the juices run clear when the thickest part of the thigh is pierced with a skewer.

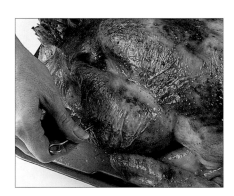

6 Transfer the turkey to a serving plate, cover it with foil and let it stand for 15 minutes before carving. To make the gravy, spoon off the fat from the roasting pan, leaving the meat juices. Blend in the flour and cook for 2 minutes. Gradually stir in the stock and bring to the boil. Check the seasoning and pour into a sauce boat.

7 To serve the turkey, remove the skewer and pour any juices into the gravy. Surround the turkey with chipolata sausages and stuffing and carve it at the table.

Duck with Plum Sauce

This is an updated version of an old English dish, which is quite quick to prepare and cook, and ideal formal dinner party fare. Make it when plums are in season, when they will be ripe and juicy.

Serves 8

8 duck quarters
2 large red onions, finely chopped
1kg/2¼lb ripe plums, stoned
*   and quartered*
60ml/4 tbsp redcurrant jelly
salt and ground black pepper

COOK'S TIP

It is important that the plums used in this dish are very ripe, otherwise the mixture will be too dry and the sauce will be extremely tart.

1 Prick the duck skin all over with a fork to release the fat during cooking and help give a crisp result, then place the portions in a heavy frying pan, skin sides down.

2 Cook the duck pieces for 10 minutes on each side, or until golden brown and cooked right through. Remove the duck from the frying pan using a slotted spoon, and keep warm.

3 Pour away all but 30ml/2 tbsp of the duck fat, then stir-fry the onion for 5 minutes, or until golden. Add the plums and cook for a further 5 minutes, stirring frequently. Add the redcurrant jelly and mix well.

4 Replace the duck portions and cook for a further 5 minutes, or until thoroughly reheated. Season with salt and pepper to taste before serving.

Wild Duck with Olives

Compared to farmed duck, wild duck, which has a brilliant flavour, is worth the extra expense for a special occasion meal. They are often quite small birds, so allow two pieces per portion. Mashed parsnips and green vegetables are good accompaniments.

Serves 4

2 wild ducks, weighing about 1.5kg/
   3¼lb, each cut into 4 pieces
2 onions, chopped
2 carrots, chopped
4 celery sticks, chopped
6 garlic cloves, sliced
2 bottles red wine
600ml/1 pint/2½ cups well-flavoured
   game stock
handful of fresh thyme leaves
5ml/1 tsp arrowroot
450g/1lb/4 cups pitted green olives
225g/8oz passata (bottled
   strained tomatoes)
salt and ground black pepper

1 Preheat the oven to 220°C/425°F/ Gas 7. Season the duck pieces generously with salt and ground black pepper and place them in a large flameproof casserole.

2 Roast the duck pieces for 25–30 minutes, then remove the casserole from the oven. Use a slotted spoon to remove the duck from the casserole, reserving the cooking fat, and set aside. Reduce the oven temperature to 160°C/325°F/Gas 3.

3 Carefully transfer the casserole to the stove and heat the duck fat until it is sizzling. Add the chopped onions, carrots, celery sticks and garlic cloves, and cook for 10 minutes, or until the vegetables are softened. Pour in the red wine and boil until it has reduced by about half.

4 Add the stock and thyme leaves, then replace the duck in the casserole. Bring to the boil, skim the surface, then cover the casserole and place in the oven for about 1 hour, or until the duck is tender. Remove the duck portions and keep warm.

5 Skim the excess fat from the cooking liquid, strain it and return it to the casserole, then bring it to the boil. Skim the liquid again, if necessary.

VARIATION
Process 225g/8oz canned tomatoes in a blender and use instead of the passata.

6 Mix the arrowroot to a thin paste with a little cold water and whisk it into the simmering sauce. Add the olives and passata and replace the duck, then cook, uncovered, for 15 minutes. Check the seasoning and serve.

eating outdoors

Discover great dishes for making barbecues
and *al fresco* eating as delicious and easy
as they are fun and informal.

Summer Vegetables with Yogurt Pesto

Chargrilled summer vegetables make a meal on their own, or are delicious served as a Mediterranean-style accompaniment to grilled meats and fish.

Serves 8

4 small aubergines (eggplant)
4 large courgettes (zucchini)
2 red (bell) peppers
2 yellow (bell) peppers
2 fennel bulbs
2 red onions
300ml/½ pint/1¼ cups Greek
   (US strained plain) yogurt
90ml/6 tbsp pesto
olive oil, for brushing
salt and ground black pepper

1 Cut the aubergines into 1cm/½in slices. Sprinkle with salt and leave to drain for about 30 minutes. Rinse well in cold running water and pat dry.

2 Use a sharp kitchen knife to cut the courgettes in half lengthways. Cut the peppers in half, removing the seeds but leaving the stalks in place.

3 Slice the fennel bulbs and the red onions into thick wedges, using a sharp kitchen knife.

4 Prepare the barbecue. Stir the yogurt and pesto lightly together in a bowl, to make a marbled sauce. Spoon the yogurt pesto into a serving bowl and set aside.

5 Arrange the vegetables on the hot barbecue, brush generously with olive oil and sprinkle with plenty of salt and ground black pepper.

6 Cook the vegetables until golden brown and tender, turning occasionally. The aubergines and peppers will take 6–8 minutes to cook, the courgettes, onion and fennel 4–5 minutes. Serve the vegetables as soon as they are cooked, with the yogurt pesto.

COOK'S TIP
Baby vegetables are excellent for grilling whole on the barbecue, so look out for baby aubergines (eggplant) and (bell) peppers, in particular. There's no need to salt the aubergines if they are small.

Moroccan Grilled Fish Brochettes

Serve these delicious skewers with strips of red peppers, potatoes and aubergine slices, which can also be cooked on the barbecue. Accompany them with warm, soft flour tortillas.

Serves 6

5 garlic cloves, chopped
2.5ml/½ tsp paprika
2.5ml/½ tsp ground cumin
2.5–5ml/½–1 tsp salt
2–3 pinches of cayenne pepper
60ml/4 tbsp olive oil
30ml/2 tbsp lemon juice
30ml/2 tbsp chopped fresh coriander (cilantro) or parsley
675g/1½lb firm-fleshed white fish, such as haddock, halibut, sea bass or snapper, cut into 2.5–5cm/ 1–2in cubes
3–4 green (bell) peppers, cut into 2.5–5cm/1–2in pieces
2 lemon wedges, to serve

1 Put the garlic, paprika, cumin, salt, cayenne pepper, oil, lemon juice and coriander or parsley in a large bowl and mix together.

2 Add the fish and toss to coat. Leave to marinate for at least 30 minutes, and preferably 2 hours, at room temperature, or chill overnight.

COOK'S TIP
If you are using wooden skewers, soak them in cold water for 30 minutes before using to stop them burning.

3 Thread the fish cubes and pepper pieces alternately on to six wooden or metal skewers.

4 About 40 minutes before you are going to cook the brochettes, prepare and light the barbecue. It will be ready when the flames subside and the coals have turned white and grey.

5 Grill the brochettes on the barbecue for 2–3 minutes on each side, or until the fish is tender and lightly browned. Serve with lemon wedges.

Grilled Squid Stuffed with Feta Cheese

A large, fresh leafy salad or a vegetable dish, such as fresh green beans with tomato sauce could be served with the grilled squid.

Serves 8

8 medium squid, total weight
    about 900g/2lb
8–12 finger-length slices of feta cheese
175ml/6fl oz/¾ cup olive oil
4 garlic cloves, crushed
6–8 fresh marjoram sprigs, leaves
    removed and chopped
salt and ground black pepper
lemon wedges, to serve

1 To prepare the squid: wash the squid carefully. If there is any ink on the body, rinse it off so that you can see what you are doing. Holding the body firmly, pull away the head and tentacles. If the ink sac is still intact, remove it. Either keep it for cooking or discard it.

2 Pull out all the innards, including the long transparent stick or "pen". Peel off and discard the thin purple skin on the body, but keep the two small fins on the sides, if desired. Slice the head across just under the eyes, severing the tentacles. Discard the rest of the squid's head. Squeeze the tentacles at the head end to push out the round beak in the centre. Throw this away. Rinse the pouch inside and out and the tentacles very thoroughly under cold running water. Drain well and pat dry on kitchen paper.

3 Lay the squid bodies and tentacles in a large shallow dish that will hold them in a single layer. Tuck the pieces of cheese between the squid.

4 To make the marinade, pour the olive oil into a jug (pitcher) or bowl and whisk in the fresh garlic and marjoram sprigs. Season to taste with salt and pepper. Pour the marinade over the squid and the cheese, then cover with foil and leave in a cool place to marinate for 2–3 hours to allow the flavours to develop, turning once.

5 Insert one or two pieces of cheese and a few bits of marjoram from the marinade into each squid and place them in a lightly oiled grill (broiler) pan or tray. Thread the tentacles on to wooden skewers that have been soaked in water for half an hour (this prevents them from burning).

6 Preheat the grill to a low setting or prepare a barbecue. Grill the stuffed squid for about 6 minutes, then turn them over. Grill them for 1–2 minutes more, then add the skewered tentacles. Grill them for 2 minutes on each side, until they start to scorch. Serve the stuffed squid with the tentacles and serve with a few lemon wedges.

COOK'S TIP
Tentacles are often left whole for frying, but can be chopped into short lengths.

Seared Tuna Steaks with Red Onion Salsa

Red onions are ideal for this salsa, not only for their mild and sweet flavour, but also because they look so appetizing. Salad, rice or bread and a bowl of thick yogurt flavoured with chopped fresh herbs are good accompaniments.

Serves 8

8 tuna loin steaks, about
    175–200g/6–7oz each
10ml/2 tsp cumin seeds, toasted
    and crushed
pinch of dried red chilli flakes
grated rind and juice of 2 limes
60–75ml/4–5 tbsp extra virgin
    olive oil
salt and ground black pepper
lime wedges and fresh coriander
    (cilantro) sprigs, to garnish

For the salsa
2 small red onions, finely chopped
400g/14oz red or yellow cherry
    tomatoes, roughly chopped
2 avocados, peeled, stoned, (pitted)
    and chopped
4 kiwi fruit, peeled and chopped
2 fresh red chillies, seeded and finely
    chopped
25g/1oz/½ cup chopped fresh
    coriander (cilantro)
12 fresh mint sprigs, leaves
    only, chopped
10–15ml/2–3 tsp Thai fish sauce
    (nam pla)
about 10ml/2 tsp muscovado
    (molasses) sugar

1 Wash the tuna steaks and pat dry. Sprinkle with half the cumin, the dried chilli flakes, salt, pepper and half the lime rind. Rub in 60ml/4 tbsp of the oil and set aside in a dish for about 30 minutes.

COOK'S TIP
The spicy fruity salsa also goes well with barbecued salmon steaks.

2 Meanwhile, make the salsa. Mix the onions, tomatoes, avocados, kiwi fruit, fresh chilli, chopped coriander and mint. Add the remaining cumin, the rest of the lime rind and half the lime juice. Add Thai fish sauce and sugar to taste. Set aside for 15–20 minutes, then add more Thai fish sauce, lime juice and olive oil if required.

3 Heat a griddle. Cook the tuna, allowing about 2 minutes on each side for rare tuna or a little longer for a medium result.

4 Serve the tuna steaks garnished with lime wedges and coriander sprigs. Serve the salsa separately or spoon it next to the tuna.

Garlic and Chilli Marinated Beef with Corn-crusted Onion Rings

Fruity, smoky and mild Mexican chillies combine well with garlic in this marinade for grilled steak.

Serves 8

40g/1½oz large mild dried red chillies, such as mulato or pasilla
4 garlic cloves, plain or smoked, finely chopped
10ml/2 tsp ground toasted cumin seeds
10ml/2 tsp dried oregano
120ml/4fl oz/½ cup olive oil
8 beef steaks, rump or rib-eye (round), 175–225g/6–8oz each
salt and ground black pepper

For the onion rings

4 onions, sliced into rings
475ml/16fl oz/2 cups milk
175g/6oz/1½ cup coarse corn meal
5ml/1 tsp dried red chilli flakes
10ml/2 tsp ground toasted cumin seeds
10ml/2 tsp dried oregano
vegetable oil, for deep-frying

1 Cut the stalks from the chillies and discard the seeds. Toast the chillies in a dry frying pan for 2–4 minutes. Place them in a bowl, cover with warm water and leave to soak for 20–30 minutes. Drain and reserve the water.

2 Process the chillies to a paste with the garlic, cumin, oregano and oil in a food processor. Add a little soaking water, if needed. Season with pepper.

3 Wash and dry the steaks, drizzle the chilli paste all over them and leave to marinate for up to 12 hours.

4 For the onion rings, soak the onions in the milk for 30 minutes. Mix the corn meal, chilli, cumin and oregano and season with salt and pepper.

5 Heat the oil for deep-frying to 160–180°C/325–350°F, or until a cube of day-old bread turns brown in about 60 seconds.

6 Drain the onion rings and dip each one into the corn meal mixture, coating it thoroughly. Fry for 2–4 minutes, or until browned and crisp. Do not overcrowd the pan, but cook in batches. Lift the onion rings out of the pan with a slotted spoon and drain on kitchen paper.

7 Heat a barbecue or griddle. Season the steaks with salt and cook for about 4 minutes on each side for a medium result.

Lamb Burgers with Red Onion and Tomato Relish

A sharp-sweet red onion relish works well with burgers based on Middle-Eastern style lamb. The burgers can be made a day ahead and chilled. Serve them with pitta bread and tabbouleh or a crisp green salad.

Serves 8

50g/2oz/⅓ cup bulgur wheat
1kg/2¼lb lean minced (ground) lamb
2 small red onions, finely chopped
4 garlic cloves, finely chopped
2 green chillies, seeded and
   finely chopped
10ml/2 tsp ground toasted cumin seeds
5ml/1 tsp ground sumac
25g/1oz/½ cup chopped fresh flat
   leaf parsley
60ml/4 tbsp chopped fresh mint
olive oil, for frying
salt and ground black pepper

For the relish
4 red (bell) peppers, halved
   and seeded
4 red onions, cut into 5mm/¼in
   thick slices
150ml/¼ pint/⅔ cup olive oil
700g/1lb 9oz cherry tomatoes, chopped
1 fresh red or green chilli, seeded and
   finely chopped (optional)
60ml/4 tbsp chopped fresh mint
60ml/4 tbsp chopped fresh parsley
30ml/2 tbsp chopped fresh oregano
   or marjoram
5ml/1 tsp ground toasted cumin seeds
5ml/1 tsp ground sumac
juice of 1 lemon
caster (superfine) sugar, to taste

1 Pour 300ml/½ pint/1¼ cups hot water over the bulgur wheat in a bowl and leave to stand for 15 minutes, then drain in a sieve and squeeze out the excess moisture.

2 Place the bulgur wheat in a bowl and add the minced lamb, onion, garlic, chilli, cumin, sumac, parsley and mint. Mix the ingredients thoroughly together by hand, then season with 10ml/2 tsp salt and plenty of black pepper and mix again. Form the mixture into 16 small burgers and set aside while you make the relish.

3 Grill (broil) the peppers, skin side up, until the skin chars and blisters. Place in a bowl, cover and leave to stand until cool. Peel off the skin, dice the peppers finely and place in a bowl.

4 Brush the onions with 30ml/2 tbsp oil and grill for 5 minutes on each side, until browned. Cool, then chop.

5 Add the onions, tomatoes, chilli (if using) to taste, the mint, parsley, oregano or marjoram and half of the cumin and sumac to the peppers. Stir in the remaining oil and 30ml/2 tbsp of the lemon juice. Season with salt, pepper and sugar and allow to stand for 20–30 minutes.

6 Prepare a barbecue or heat a heavy frying pan or griddle over a high heat and grease with olive oil. Cook the burgers for about 5–6 minutes on each side, or until just cooked at the centre.

7 While the burgers are cooking, taste the relish and adjust the seasoning, adding more salt, pepper, sugar, chilli, cumin, sumac and lemon juice to taste. Serve the burgers as soon as they are cooked, with the relish.

Barbecued Chicken

A fragrant marinade of Thai spices and coconut gives this barbecued chicken a superb flavour. It makes ideal party food for outdoor eating with a difference.

Serves 6

1 chicken, about 1.5kg/3¼lb, cut into
  8–10 pieces
lime wedges and fresh red chillies,
  to garnish

For the marinade
2 lemon grass stalks, roots removed
2.5cm/1in piece fresh root ginger,
  peeled and thinly sliced
6 garlic cloves, roughly chopped
4 shallots, roughly chopped
½ bunch coriander (cilantro)
  roots, chopped
15ml/1 tbsp palm sugar
120ml/4fl oz/½ cup coconut milk
30ml/2 tbsp Thai fish sauce (nam pla)
30ml/2 tbsp light soy sauce

1 To make the marinade, cut off the lower 5cm/2in of both of the lemon grass stalks and chop them roughly. Put into a food processor or blender along with all the other marinade ingredients and process until the mixture has reached a smooth consistency.

COOK'S TIP
You can buy coconut milk fresh, in cans or cartons, or use 50g/2oz creamed coconut, available in packets, and dissolve in 120ml/4fl oz/½ cup warm water.

2 Place the chicken pieces in a fairly deep dish, pour over the marinade and stir to mix well, turning the chicken pieces over. Cover the dish and leave in a cool place to marinate for at least 4 hours or place the dish in the refrigerator if you leave the chicken to stand overnight.

3 Prepare the barbecue. Grill the chicken over the barbecue for 20–30 minutes, or until the pieces are cooked and golden brown. Turn the pieces and brush with the marinade once or twice during cooking. Transfer to a serving platter and garnish with lime wedges and red chillies to serve.

Turkey Patties

Minced turkey makes deliciously light patties, which are ideal for summer meals. Serve the patties in split and toasted buns or between thick pieces of crusty bread, with chutney, salad leaves and chunky fries or potato wedges.

Serves 6

675g/1½lb minced (ground) turkey
1 small red onion, finely chopped
grated rind and juice of 1 lime
small handful of fresh thyme leaves
15–30ml/1–2 tbsp olive oil
salt and ground black pepper

1 Mix together the turkey, onion, lime rind and juice, thyme and seasoning. Cover and chill for up to 4 hours to allow the flavours to infuse (steep), then divide the mixture into six equal portions and shape into round patties.

2 Preheat a griddle. Brush the patties with oil, then place them on the griddle and cook for 10–12 minutes. Turn the patties over, brush with more oil and cook for 10–12 minutes on the second side, or until cooked through.

Herbed Greek Tartlets

Mixed fresh herbs give these little tarts a delicate flavour.

Makes 8

*45–60ml/3–4 tbsp tapenade or sun-
    dried tomato purée (paste)*
1 large (US extra large) egg
*100g/3¾oz/scant ½ cup thick Greek
    (US strained plain) yogurt*
90ml/6 tbsp milk
1 garlic clove, crushed
*30ml/2 tbsp chopped mixed herbs,
    such as thyme, basil and parsley*
salt and ground black pepper

For the pastry
115g/4oz/1 cup plain (all-purpose) flour
50g/2oz/4 tbsp butter, diced
15–25ml/1–1½ tbsp water

1 To make the pastry, mix together the flour, a pinch of salt and the butter. Using the fingertips or a pastry cutter, rub the butter into the flour until the mixture resembles fine breadcrumbs. Mix in the water using a round-bladed knife and knead lightly to form a firm dough. Wrap the dough in clear film (plastic wrap) and chill in the refrigerator for 30 minutes.

2 Preheat the oven to 190°C/375°F/Gas 5. Roll out the pastry thinly and cut out eight rounds using a 7.5cm/3in cutter. Line deep patty tins (muffin pans) with the pastry rounds, then line each one with a small piece of baking parchment. Bake blind for 15 minutes. Remove the baking parchment and cook for a further 5 minutes, or until the cases are crisp.

3 Spread a little tapenade or tomato purée in the base of each pastry case. Whisk together the egg, yogurt, milk, garlic, herbs and seasoning. Spoon carefully into the pastry cases and bake for 25–30 minutes, or until the filling is just firm and the pastry golden. Allow the tarts to cool slightly before carefully removing from the tins and serving.

Tomato and Black Olive Tart

This delicious tart has a fresh, rich Mediterranean flavour and is ideal for picnics and buffets. Using a rectangular tin makes the tart easier to transport and divide into portions.

Serves 8

3 eggs, beaten
300ml/½ pint/1¼ cups milk
*30ml/2 tbsp chopped fresh herbs,
    such as parsley, marjoram or basil*
6 firm plum tomatoes
75g/3oz ripe Brie
about 16 black olives, pitted
salt and ground black pepper

For the pastry
*250g/9oz/1 cup plain (all-purpose)
    flour, plus extra for dusting*
2.5ml/½ tsp salt
130g/4½oz/1 cup butter, diced
45ml/3 tbsp water

1 Preheat the oven to 190°C/375°F/ Gas 5. To make the pastry, mix together the flour, salt and butter. Using the fingertips or a pastry cutter, rub the butter into the flour until the mixture resembles fine breadcrumbs. Mix in the water and knead lightly to form a firm dough. Roll out the pastry thinly on a lightly floured surface. Line a 28 × 18cm/11 × 7in loose-based rectangular flan tin (quiche pan), trimming off any overhanging edges.

2 Line the pastry case with baking parchment and baking beans, and bake blind for 15 minutes. Remove the baking parchment and baking beans and bake for a further 5 minutes, or until the base is crisp.

VARIATION
This tart is delicious made with other cheeses. Try slices of Gorgonzola or Camembert for a slightly stronger flavour.

3 Meanwhile, beat the eggs with the milk, seasoning and herbs. Slice the tomatoes thinly, cube the cheese, and slice the olives. Place the prepared flan case on a baking tray, arrange the tomatoes, cheese and olives in the bottom of the case, then pour over the egg mixture.

4 Transfer the tart carefully to the oven and bake for about 40 minutes, or until the filling is just firm and turning golden. Serve the tart warm or cold, cut into slices.

Summer Herb Ricotta Flan

Infused with aromatic herbs, this flan makes a delightful picnic dish.

Serves 8

olive oil, for greasing and glazing
800g/1³/₄lb/3½ cups ricotta cheese
75g/3oz/1 cup grated Parmesan cheese
3 eggs, separated
60ml/4 tbsp torn fresh basil leaves
60ml/4 tbsp chopped fresh chives
45ml/3 tbsp fresh oregano leaves
2.5ml/½ tsp paprika
salt and ground black pepper
fresh herb leaves, to garnish

For the tapenade
400g/14oz/3½ cups pitted black olives,
  rinsed and halved, reserving a few
  whole to garnish (optional)
5 garlic cloves, crushed
75ml/5 tbsp olive oil

1 Preheat the oven to 180°C/350°F/ Gas 4 and lightly grease a 23cm/9in springform cake tin (pan) with oil. Mix together the ricotta cheese, Parmesan and egg yolks in a food processor or blender. Add the herbs and seasoning, and blend until smooth and creamy.

2 Whisk the egg whites in a large bowl until they form soft peaks. Gently fold the egg whites into the ricotta cheese mixture using a rubber spatula, taking care not to knock out too much air. Spoon the ricotta mixture into the prepared tin and smooth the top.

3 Bake for 1 hour 20 minutes or until the flan is risen and the top is golden. Remove from the oven and brush lightly with olive oil, then sprinkle with paprika. Leave the flan to cool before removing from the pan.

4 Make the tapenade. Place the olives and garlic in a food processor or blender and process until finely chopped. Gradually add the olive oil and blend to a coarse paste, then transfer to a serving bowl. Garnish the flan with fresh herbs leaves and serve with the tapenade.

VARIATION
Sprinkle 25g/1oz chopped, drained sun-dried tomatoes over the flan as a garnish.

Red Onion and Goat's Cheese Pastries

These attractive little pastries are ideal for picnics and summer buffets and couldn't be easier to make. Serve simply with a mixed green salad dressed with balsamic vinegar and extra-virgin olive oil.

Serves 8

30ml/2 tbsp olive oil
900g/2lb red onions, sliced
60ml/4 tbsp fresh thyme or
  20ml/4 tsp dried
30ml/2 tbsp balsamic vinegar
850g/1lb 14oz ready-rolled puff pastry
225g/8oz/1 cup goat's cheese, cubed
2 eggs, beaten
salt and ground black pepper
fresh thyme sprigs, to garnish
  (optional)
mixed green salad leaves and
  cherry tomatoes, to serve

1 Heat the olive oil in a large heavy frying pan, add the sliced red onions and fry over a gentle heat for 10 minutes or until softened, stirring occasionally with a wooden spoon to prevent them browning.

2 Add the thyme, seasoning and balsamic vinegar, and cook the onions for a further 5 minutes. Remove the frying pan from the heat and leave to cool.

3 Preheat the oven to 220°C/425°F/ Gas 7. Unroll the puff pastry and using a 15cm/6in plate as a guide, cut out eight equal rounds. Place the pastry rounds on dampened baking sheets and, using the point of a sharp knife, score a border, 2cm/¾in inside the edge of each round.

4 Divide the onions among the pastry rounds and top with the goat's cheese. Brush the edge of each round with beaten egg and bake for 25–30 minutes until golden. Garnish with thyme, if using, before serving with the salad leaves and tomatoes.

VARIATION
Ring the changes by spreading the pastry base with 45ml/3 tbsp pesto or tapenade (see recipe above) before you add the onion filling.

diva desserts

Ensure that your guests leave the party on a
high note after sampling one (or more!) of these
superlative, mouthwatering sweet dishes.

Summer Berries in **Warm Sabayon Glaze**

This luxurious combination of summer berries under a light and fluffy alcoholic sauce is lightly grilled to form a deliciously crisp, caramelized topping.

Serves 8

900g/2lb/8 cups mixed summer berries, or soft fruit

8 egg yolks

115g/4oz/generous ½ cup vanilla sugar or caster (superfine) sugar

250ml/8fl oz/1 cup liqueur, such as Cointreau, Kirsch or Grand Marnier, or white dessert wine, plus extra for drizzling (optional)

a little icing (confectioners') sugar, sifted, and mint leaves, to decorate (optional)

1 Divide the fruit among eight individual heatproof glass dishes or ramekins. Preheat the grill (broiler).

2 Whisk the yolks in a large heatproof bowl with the sugar and liqueur or wine. Place the bowl over a pan of hot boiling water and whisk constantly until the yolks have become thick, fluffy and pale.

3 Pour equal quantities of the sauce into each dish. Place under the grill for 1–2 minutes, or until just turning brown. Sprinkle the fruit with icing sugar and scatter with mint leaves just before serving, if you like.

COOK'S TIP

To omit the alcohol, use a juice substitute such as grape, mango or apricot.

Fig, Port and Clementine Sundaes

These exotic sundaes will make an ideal finale to a rich meal. The fresh flavours of figs and clementines contrast beautifully with the warm spices and port.

Serves 6

6 clementines
30ml/2 tbsp clear honey
1 cinnamon stick, halved
15ml/1 tbsp light muscovado
*   (brown) sugar*
60ml/4 tbsp port
6 fresh figs
about 500ml/17fl oz/2¼ cups orange
*   sorbet (sherbet)*

1 Finely grate the rind from two clementines and put it in a small, heavy pan. Cut the peel off the clementines, then slice the flesh thinly. Add the honey, cinnamon, sugar and port to the rind. Heat gently until the sugar has dissolved, to make a syrup.

2 Put the clementine slices in a heatproof bowl and pour over the syrup. Cool completely, then chill.

3 Slice the figs thinly and add to the clementines and syrup, tossing the ingredients together gently. Leave to stand for 10 minutes, then discard the cinnamon stick.

4 Arrange half the fig and clementine slices around the sides of six serving glasses. Half fill the glasses with scoops of sorbet. Arrange the remaining fruit slices around the sides of the glasses, then pile more sorbet into the centre. Pour over the port syrup and serve.

COOK'S TIPS
A variety of different types of fresh figs are available. Dark purple skinned figs have a deep red flesh; yellowy-green figs have a pink flesh and green skinned figs have an amber coloured flesh. All types can be eaten, complete with the skin, simply as they are or baked and served with Greek (US strained plain) yogurt and honey for a quick dessert. When they are ripe, you can split them open with your fingers to reveal the soft, sweet flesh full of edible seeds.

Classic Lemon Tart

This citrus tart can be served warm or chilled and would be suitable for a formal dinner party or a buffet. It is very lemony, so serve with cream or vanilla ice cream.

Serves 8

150g/5oz/1¼ cups plain (all-purpose) flour, sifted

50g/2oz/½ cup hazelnuts, toasted and finely ground

175g/6oz/scant 1 cup caster (superfine) sugar

115g/4oz/½ cup unsalted (sweet) butter, softened

4 eggs

finely grated rind of 2 lemons and at least 175ml/6fl oz/¾ cup lemon juice

150ml/¼ pint/⅔ cup double (heavy) cream

thinly pared and shredded lemon rind, to decorate

1 Mix together the flour, nuts and 25g/1oz/2 tbsp sugar, then gently work in the butter and, if necessary, 15–30ml/1–2 tbsp cold water to make a soft dough. Chill for 10 minutes.

2 Roll out the dough and use to line a 20cm/8in loose-based flan tin (tart pan). If you find it too difficult to roll out, gently press the pastry into the flan tin working it up the sides. Chill for about 20 minutes. Preheat the oven to 200°C/400°F/Gas 6.

3 Line the pastry case with baking parchment, fill with baking beans, and bake for 15 minutes. Remove the baking parchment and baking beans, and cook for a further 5–10 minutes, or until the base is crisp.

4 Beat the eggs, lemon rind and juice, the remaining sugar and cream until well blended. Pour into the pastry case. Bake for about 30 minutes, or until just set. Turn out of the tin, decorate with the lemon rind and serve.

Boston Banoffee Pie

This is a simple but impressive party dish. You can press the wonderfully biscuity pastry into the tin, rather than rolling it out. You can make the pastry case and the fudge-toffee filling in advance and then arrange the sliced banana topping and cream before serving. It will prove irresistible.

Serves 6

115g/4oz/½ cup butter, diced
200g/7oz can skimmed, sweetened
* condensed milk*
115g/4oz/½ cup soft brown sugar
30ml/2 tbsp golden (light corn) syrup
2 small bananas, sliced
a little lemon juice
whipped cream, to decorate
5ml/1 tsp grated plain
* (semisweet) chocolate*

For the pastry
150g/5oz/1¼ cups plain
* (all-purpose) flour*
115g/4oz/½ cup butter, diced
50g/2oz/¼ cup caster
* (superfine) sugar*

1 Preheat the oven to 160°C/325°F/ Gas 3. In a food processor, process the flour and diced butter until crumbed. Stir in the caster sugar and mix to form a soft, pliable dough.

2 Press the dough into a 20cm/8in loose-based flan tin (quiche pan). Bake for 30 minutes.

3 To make the filling, place the butter in a pan with the condensed milk, brown sugar and syrup. Heat gently, stirring, until the butter has melted and the sugar has completely dissolved.

4 Bring to a gentle boil and cook for 7–10 minutes, stirring constantly, until the mixture thickens and turns a light caramel colour.

5 Pour the hot caramel filling into the pastry case and leave until it is completely cold. Sprinkle the banana slices with lemon juice to stop them going brown and arrange them in overlapping circles on top of the filling, leaving a gap in the centre. Pipe a generous swirl of whipped cream in the centre and sprinkle with the grated chocolate.

Passion Fruit Crème Caramels with Dipped Physalis

The aromatic flavour of the fruit permeates these crème caramels, which are perfect for a dinner party.

Serves 8

375g/13oz/generous 1¾ cups caster (superfine) sugar
150ml/¼ pint/⅔ cup water
8 passion fruit
8 physalis
6 eggs plus 2 egg yolks
300ml/½ pint/1¼ cups double (heavy) cream
300ml/½ pint/1¼ cups full cream (whole) milk

1 Place 300g/11oz/1½ cups of the caster sugar in a heavy pan. Add the water and heat the mixture gently until the sugar has dissolved. Increase the heat and boil until the syrup turns a dark golden colour.

2 Meanwhile, cut each passion fruit in half. Scoop out the seeds from the passion fruit into a sieve set over a bowl. Press the seeds against the sieve to extract all their juice. Spoon a few of the seeds into each of eight 150ml/ ¼ pint/⅔ cup ramekins. Reserve the passion fruit juice.

3 Peel back the papery casing from each physalis and dip the orange berries into the caramel. Place on a sheet of baking parchment and set aside. Pour the remaining caramel carefully into the ramekins.

4 Preheat the oven to 150°C/300°F/ Gas 2. Whisk the eggs, egg yolks and remaining sugar in a bowl. Whisk in the cream and milk, then the passion fruit juice. Strain through a sieve into each ramekin, then place the ramekins in a baking tin (pan). Pour in hot water to come halfway up the sides of the dishes and bake for 40–45 minutes, or until just set.

5 Remove the custards from the tin and leave to cool, then cover and chill them for 4 hours before serving. Run a knife between the edge of each ramekin and the custard and invert each in turn on to a dessert plate. Shake the ramekins firmly to release the custards before lifting them off the desserts. Decorate each with a dipped physalis.

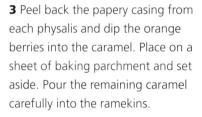

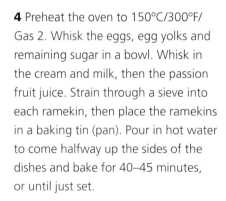

Frozen Grand Marnier Soufflés

2 Heat the milk until almost boiling and pour it on to the yolks, whisking constantly. Return to the pan and stir over a gentle heat until the custard is thick enough to coat the back of the spoon. Remove the pan from the heat. Stir the soaked gelatine into the custard. Pour the custard into a bowl and leave to cool. Whisk occasionally, until on the point of setting.

3 Put the remaining sugar in a pan with 45ml/3 tbsp water and dissolve it over a low heat. Bring to the boil and boil rapidly until it reaches the soft ball stage or 119°C/238°F on a sugar thermometer. Remove from the heat. In a clean bowl, whisk the egg whites until stiff. Pour the hot syrup on to the whites, whisking constantly. Leave the meringue to cool.

4 Add the Grand Marnier to the cold custard. Whisk the cream until it holds soft peaks and fold into the cooled meringue, with the custard. Pour into the prepared glasses or dishes. Freeze overnight. Remove the paper collars and leave at room temperature for 15 minutes before serving.

Light and fluffy yet almost ice cream, these delicious soufflés are perfect and wonderfully easy for a special dinner. Start preparations the day before as the desserts have to be frozen overnight.

Serves 8

200g/7oz/1 cup caster (superfine) sugar
6 large (US extra large) eggs,
  separated
250ml/8fl oz/1 cup milk
15ml/1 tbsp powdered gelatine,
  soaked in 45ml/3 tbsp cold water
60ml/4 tbsp Grand Marnier
450ml/¾ pint/scant 2 cups double
  (heavy) cream

1 Wrap a double collar of baking parchment around eight dessert glasses or ramekin dishes and tie with string. Whisk together 75g/3oz/scant ½ cup of the caster sugar with the egg yolks, until the yolks are pale. This will take about 5 minutes by hand or about 3 minutes with an electric hand mixer.

COOK'S TIPS
• The soft ball stage of a syrup is when a teaspoon of the mixture dropped into a glass of cold water sets into a ball.
• If you prefer, you can make just one dessert in a large soufflé dish, rather than eight individual ones, or serve in very small glasses for a buffet.

Cold Lemon Soufflé with Almonds

Terrific to look at yet easy to make, this dessert is mouthwatering, ideal for the end of any party meal.

Serves 6

oil, for greasing
grated rind and juice of 3 large lemons
5 large (US extra large) eggs, separated
115g/4oz/generous ½ cup caster
  (superfine) sugar
25ml/1½ tbsp powdered gelatine
450ml/¾ pint/scant 2 cups double
  (heavy) cream

For the almond topping
75g/3oz/¾ cup flaked (sliced) almonds
75g/3oz/¾ cup icing
  (confectioner's) sugar

1 To make the soufflé collar, cut a strip of baking parchment long enough to fit around a 900ml/1½ pint/3¾ cup soufflé dish and wide enough to extend 7.5cm/3in above the rim. Fit the strip around the dish, tape, and then tie it around the top of the dish with string. Using a pastry brush, lightly coat the inside of the paper collar with oil.

2 Put the lemon rind and yolks in a bowl. Add 75g/3oz/6 tbsp of the caster sugar and whisk until the mixture is creamy.

COOK'S TIP
Heat the lemon juice and gelatine in a microwave, on full power, in 30-second bursts, stirring between each burst, until it is fully dissolved.

3 Place the lemon juice in a small heatproof bowl and sprinkle over the gelatine. Set aside for 5 minutes, then place the bowl in a pan of simmering water. Heat, stirring occasionally, until the gelatine has dissolved. Cool slightly, then stir the gelatine and lemon juice into the egg yolk mixture.

4 In a separate bowl, lightly whip the cream to soft peaks. Fold into the egg yolk mixture and set aside.

5 Whisk the whites to stiff peaks. Gradually whisk in the remaining caster sugar until stiff and glossy. Quickly and lightly fold the whites into the yolk mix. Pour into the prepared dish, smooth the surface and chill for 4–5 hours.

6 To make the almond topping, brush a baking tray lightly with oil. Preheat the grill (broiler). Sprinkle the flaked almonds across the baking tray and sift the icing sugar over. Grill (broil) until the nuts turn a rich golden colour and the sugar has caramelized.

7 Allow to cool, then remove the almond mixture from the tray with a palette knife (metal spatula) and break it into pieces.

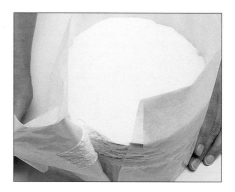

8 When the soufflé has set, carefully peel off the paper. If the paper does not come away easily, hold the blade of a knife against the set soufflé to help it keep its shape. Sprinkle the caramelized almonds over the top before serving.

VARIATIONS
• This soufflé is wonderfully refreshing when served semi-frozen. Place the undecorated, set soufflé in the freezer for about an hour. Just before serving, remove from the freezer and decorate with the caramelized almonds.
• You can also vary the flavour slightly by using the juice and rind of 5 limes.

Chocolate Chestnut Roulade

This is a dream dinner party finale to have chocoholics swooning. The combination of intense flavours produces a very rich dessert, so serve it well chilled and in thin slices. It slices better when it is cold.

Serves 10 to 12

oil, for greasing
175g/6oz dark (bittersweet)
    chocolate, chopped
30ml/2 tbsp cocoa powder
    (unsweetened), sifted,
    plus extra for dusting
50ml/2fl oz/¼ cup freshly brewed
    strong coffee or espresso
6 eggs, separated
75g/3oz/6 tbsp caster (superfine) sugar
pinch of cream of tartar
5ml/1 tsp vanilla essence (extract)
glacé (candied) chestnuts,
    to decorate (optional)

For the chestnut cream filling
475ml/16fl oz/2 cups double
    (heavy) cream
30ml/2 tbsp rum or coffee-
    flavoured liqueur
350g/12oz can sweetened
    chestnut purée
115g/4oz dark chocolate, grated
thick cream, to serve

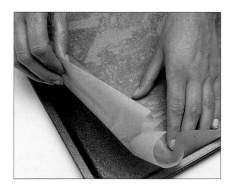

1 Preheat the oven to 180°C/350°F/Gas 4. Oil the base and sides of a 38 × 25cm/15 × 10in Swiss roll tin (jelly roll pan). Line with baking parchment, allowing a 2.5cm/1in overhang.

2 Melt the chocolate in the top of a double boiler, over a low heat, stirring frequently. Set aside. Dissolve the cocoa in the coffee. Stir to make a smooth paste. Set aside.

3 In an electric mixer or in a bowl using a whisk, beat the egg yolks with half the sugar for about 3–5 minutes, or until pale and thick. Slowly beat in the melted chocolate and cocoa-coffee paste until just blended.

4 In another bowl, beat the egg whites and cream of tartar until stiff peaks form. Sprinkle the remaining sugar over in two batches incorporating each thoroughly, and continue to beat until they are stiff and glossy. Then beat in the vanilla essence.

5 Stir a spoonful of the whisked whites into the chocolate mixture to lighten it, then fold in the remainder.

6 Spoon the mixture into the tin and level the top. Bake for 20–25 minutes, or until the cake is firm, set and risen, and springs back when lightly pressed with the fingertips.

7 Meanwhile, dust a clean dishtowel with the extra cocoa powder. As soon as the cake is cooked, carefully turn it out on to the towel and gently peel off the baking parchment from the base. Starting at a narrow end, roll the cake and towel together Swiss-roll fashion. Cool completely.

8 To make the filling, whip the cream and rum or liqueur until soft peaks form. Beat a spoonful of cream into the chestnut purée to lighten it, then fold in the remaining cream and most of the grated chocolate. Reserve a quarter of the chestnut cream mixture.

9 To assemble the roulade, unroll the cake and spread with the filling, to within 2.5cm/1in of the edges. Gently roll it up, using the towel for support.

10 Place the roulade on a serving plate. Spoon the reserved chestnut cream into a small icing bag and pipe rosettes along the top of the roulade. Dust with more cocoa and decorate with glacé chestnuts and grated chocolate.

Iced Christmas Torte

Not everyone likes traditional Christmas pudding. This makes an exciting alternative but do not feel that you have to limit it to the festive season. Packed with dried fruit and nuts, it is perfect for any special occasion.

Serves 8 to 10

75g/3oz/¾ cup dried cranberries
75g/3oz/scant ½ cup pitted prunes
50g/2oz/⅓ cup sultanas (golden raisins)
175ml/6fl oz/¾ cup port
2 pieces preserved stem ginger,
*   finely chopped*
25g/1oz/2 tbsp unsalted (sweet) butter
45ml/3 tbsp light muscovado
*   (brown) sugar*
90g/3½oz/scant 2 cups fresh
*   white breadcrumbs*
600ml/1 pint/2½ cups double
*   (heavy) cream*
30ml/2 tbsp icing (confectioners') sugar
5ml/1 tsp mixed (pumpkin pie) spice
75g/3oz/¾ cup brazil nuts,
*   finely chopped*
sugared bay leaves (see Cook's Tip)
*   and fresh cherries, to decorate*

1 Put the cranberries, prunes and sultanas in a food processor and process briefly. Tip them into a bowl and add the port and ginger. Leave to absorb the port for 2 hours.

2 Melt the butter in a frying pan. Add the sugar and heat gently until it has dissolved. Tip in the breadcrumbs, stir, then fry over a low heat for about 5 minutes, or until lightly coloured and turning crisp. Leave to cool.

COOK'S TIP
To make the sugared bay leaves wash and dry the leaves, then paint both sides with beaten egg white. Sprinkle with caster (superfine) sugar. Leave to dry on baking parchment for 2–3 hours.

3 Tip the breadcrumbs into a food processor or blender and process to finer crumbs. Sprinkle a third into an 18cm/7in loose-based springform cake tin (pan) and spread them out to cover the base of the tin evenly. Freeze until firm.

4 Whip the cream with the icing sugar and mixed spice until it is thick but not yet standing in peaks. Fold in the brazil nuts with the fruit mixture and any port that has not been absorbed.

5 Spread a third of the mixture over the breadcrumb base in the tin, taking care not to dislodge the crumbs. Sprinkle with another layer of the breadcrumbs. Repeat the layering, finishing with a layer of the cream mixture. Freeze the torte overnight.

6 Chill the torte for about 1 hour before serving, decorated with sugared bay leaves and fresh cherries.

Black Forest Gâteau

Morello cherries and Kirsch lend their distinctive flavours to this ever-popular chocolate gâteau.

Serves 8 to 10

6 eggs
200g/7oz/1 cup caster (superfine) sugar
5ml/1 tsp vanilla essence (extract)
50g/2oz/½ cup plain (all-purpose) flour
50g/2oz/½ cup cocoa powder
  (unsweetened)
115g/4oz/½ cup unsalted (sweet)
  butter, melted

For the filling and topping
60ml/4 tbsp Kirsch
600ml/1 pint/2½ cups double
  (heavy) cream
30ml/2 tbsp icing (confectioners') sugar
2.5ml/½ tsp vanilla essence (extract)
675g/1½ lb jar pitted morello cherries,
  well drained

To decorate
icing (confectioner's) sugar, for dusting
grated chocolate
chocolate curls (see Cook's Tip)
fresh or drained canned morello cherries

1 Preheat oven to 180°C/350°F/Gas 4. Grease three 19cm/7½ in sandwich cake tins (pans). Line the bottom of each with baking parchment. Combine the eggs with the sugar and vanilla essence in a bowl and beat with a hand-held electric mixer until pale and thick.

2 Sift the flour and cocoa powder over the mixture and fold in lightly and evenly with a metal spoon. Gently stir in the melted butter.

COOK'S TIP
To make chocolate curls, spread melted chocolate over a marble slab to a depth of about 5mm/¼ in. Leave to set. Draw a knife across the chocolate at a 45° angle, using a seesaw action to make long curls.

3 Divide the mixture among the prepared cake tins, smoothing them level. Bake for 15–18 minutes, or until the cakes have risen and are springy to the touch. Leave them to cool in the tins for about 5 minutes, then turn out on to wire racks and leave to cool completely. Remove the lining paper from each cake layer.

4 Prick each layer all over with a skewer or fork, then sprinkle with Kirsch. Using a hand-held electric mixer, whip the cream until it starts to thicken then beat in the icing sugar and vanilla until the mixture begins to hold its shape.

5 To assemble, spread one cake layer with a thick layer of flavoured cream and top with about half the cherries.

6 Spread a second cake layer with cream, top with the remaining cherries, then place it on top of the first layer. Top with the final cake layer.

7 Spread the remaining cream all over the cake. Dust a serving plate with icing sugar, and position the cake carefully in the centre. Press grated chocolate over the sides and decorate the top of the cake with the chocolate curls and fresh or drained cherries.

Index